# THE ULTIMATE PUBLIC SPEAKING SURVIVAL GUIDE

## 37 THINGS YOU MUST KNOW WHEN YOU START PUBLIC SPEAKING

**RAMAKRISHNA REDDY**

No part of this publication may be reproduced or transmitted in any form or by any means, mechanical or electronic, including photocopying or recording, or by any information storage and retrieval system, or transmitted by email without permission in writing from the author. However, short paragraphs can be quoted with due credit to the author.

While all attempts have been made to verify the information provided in this publication, neither the author nor the publisher assumes any responsibility for errors, omissions, or contrary interpretations of the subject matter herein.

This book is for informational purpose only. The views expressed are those of the author alone, and should not be taken as expert instruction or commands. The reader is responsible for his or her own actions.

Adherence to all applicable laws and regulations, including international, federal, state, and local governing professional licensing, business practices, advertising, and all other aspects of doing business in the US, India or any other jurisdiction is the sole responsibility of the purchaser or reader.

Any perceived slight of any individual or organization is purely unintentional.

Neither the author nor the publisher assumes any responsibility or liability whatsoever on behalf of the purchaser or reader of this material.

# ALSO BY RAMAKRISHNA REDDY

*Toastmaster's Secret*

*Public Speaking Essentials*

*Public Speaking Topic Secrets*

*Connect Using Humor and Story*

*Confessions of a Software Techie*

*Write Effective Emails at Work*

# Contents

Dedication ................................................................ ix

A Gift for You .......................................................... xi

Introduction ............................................................ xiii

Chapter 1. Psychological Barriers.......................... 1

   1. Public speaking is overwhelming. How can
   I understand it in simple terms? ........................ 1

   2. Fear strikes me whenever I want to give a
   presentation. What should I do?........................ 3

   3. What will other people think if I make a
   mistake during my presentation? ..................... 6

   4. Can I really sizzle on stage even though I don't
   have an eye-catching look? ............................... 8

   5. Even though speaking comes naturally to me, do
   I still need to prepare my presentation?........... 8

   6. Can I still give an effective presentation even
   without a strong vocabulary? ......................... 10

Chapter 2. Speech Creation.................................. 13

   7. I know my topic but I feel stuck. What am I missing?........... 13

8. How do I start creating content for my presentation?.............16

9. How do I create a killer opening for my talk?.........................19

10. What is a context setting and how do I create one?...............22

11. How do I select the key points for my presentation?............23

12. How do I support the key points of my presentation? ..........26

13. How to create a compelling story? .........................................36

14. How do I best use transitions in my speech?.........................40

15. How can I have an effective summary? ...................................44

16. How do I create a memorable conclusion
for my speech?...................................................................................45

17. How do I refine my speech content?.......................................47

**Chapter 3. Speech Delivery** ................................................... **51**

18. I know my content very well, so do I really need
to care about anything else? .........................................................51

19. How should I move during the presentation? .......................52

20. How do I make effective eye contact?....................................54

21. Is there a simple way to improve the quality of my voice?....55

22. How do I use my hands during the presentation? .................59

23. How to create correct facial expressions during the
presentation? ....................................................................................61

**Chapter 4. Preparation Steps** ........................................... **63**

24. How can I create and maintain my connection
with the audience?...........................................................................63

25. Is there a particular strategy to ensure that the
audience will continue to listen?.....................................66

26. What is the final checkpoint, before I freeze my content? .......... 69

27. Can the venue affect my presentation? .....................................70

28. Can you give me the exact steps to practice my speech?............. 73

29. Can you give me a strategy for not going blank on stage?........... 76

**Chapter 5. Presentation Day Steps** ................................. **77**

30. How to dress for my presentation?...........................................77

31. Is there a checklist for the presentation day? .........................79

32. What if my heart starts pounding, ears get heated and
hands become cold, 10 minutes before the presentation?...........81

33. How do I carry myself from seat to stage, once
the anchor calls my name? ...............................................83

34. How do I handle myself during the actual presentation?........ 84

35. How do I handle any unexpected problems during
the actual presentation? ...................................................85

36. How do I carry myself off the stage after my presentation? ....... 87

37. What should I do after the presentation?...............................88

**Bonus Chapter. Speech Script** ....................................... **93**

**Conclusion**......................................................................... **97**

**Gratitude** ......................................................................... **99**

# Dedication

To Lakshmi – my sister, philosopher and guide.

# A Gift for You

As a thank you note for purchase of this book, I'm excited to add more value. You can now:

- Quickly create speeches using 'informational' and 'persuasive' speech templates

- Learn about creating humor in 30 minutes from 'Humor Creation Made Simple' mini-book

Visit below link to get instant access to these gifts.

https://publicspeakking.com/37steps/

# Introduction

Public speaking is not an option but a necessity whether you are corporate warrior or an entrepreneur.

There are loads and loads of information about public speaking but nothing simplifies the whole process in a question and answer format.

It was precisely for this reason that I created this book.

Like my other books, this book adheres to my motto: simple to understand, easy to implement. Practical information along with proven principles is distilled into a simple to understand and easy to implement approach. The uniqueness in this book lies in its SIMPLICITY and STRUCTURE.

And the information is easy to find because it is listed under logical chapters.

My goal is simple.

I want you to succeed in public speaking. And this book is going to help you in accomplishing this goal.


Let us start this journey.

–Rama

# CHAPTER 1.

# Psychological Barriers

*In which you'll learn how to overcome the six common psychological barriers*

## 1. Public speaking is overwhelming. How can I understand it in simple terms?

Yes, public speaking is overwhelming. However, to understand it in simple terms let me start with a simple question: Do you drive a vehicle?

Public speaking is like driving a vehicle full of passengers to their destination. Do not get carried away with the simplicity of that statement before you understand that the word "vehicle" is correlated to speech content, "passengers" is correlated to speech audience and "destination" to speech objective. The stage setting is the road being traveled and your speech delivery equates to your driving skill.

The first time you drove – did you switch on the car, change the gear, accelerate and drive on the freeway? I hope you said, "No." How was that first experience when you learnt to drive? I am sure you felt overwhelmed even before starting the car. Similarly, starting to speak in front of an audience can be overwhelming. It is just natural.

With driving, you start off learning primary activities such as acceleration, applying brakes, changing gears, maybe using the clutch, steering, etc., as separate skills. Similarly, in public speaking, the primary elements, such as content creation, eye contact, voice modulation, hand gestures, facial expressions, stance, movement, etc., are also learnt as separate skills.

In driving, I am pretty sure you had to drive X number of miles to learn to perform the primary functions in a smooth manner. To illustrate better, you start the vehicle, then you look out on the road and at the same time you change gears, press down on the accelerator and steer, and you are finally rocking down the road. Even in public speaking, after you speak X number of times, you will need to have your voice modulated, proper eye contact with your audience, gestures worked out and maybe a few other things, all working in unison before you are rocking on the stage.

In order to make the drive interesting and enjoyable for you and your passengers, you can equip your vehicle with a stereo system, adjustable seats, food and much more. Even when speaking, you can tell stories, create humor and use visual aids along with other things to keep the presentation interesting and enjoyable.

In driving context, you and your passengers experience the journey. In public speaking, you and your audience also experience the journey. The similarity in these two activities comes in the same way.

In the case of driving, unless you know where you are going, you waste not only your time, but that of your passengers. Similarly, if you are unprepared when making a presentation, you waste your time and your audience's time as well. If you do not have a purpose in mind before you start to speak, you won't know how you want your audience to act, think or feel after your presentation, whereas you should.

As every drive has a purpose, similarly every public speaking presentation also has a purpose. Now for example, your drive to work is important. In this case, you ideally would not stop and while away time on leisure activities. But if you are on a long recreational drive, you can stop, have fun and spend time on leisure activities. Similarly, public speaking presentations have different purposes. For example, your purpose could be *to inform* your audience (a technical presentation), *to entertain* your audience (an after-dinner speech) or *to persuade* your audience (a sales presentation). However, there can be deviations. For example, maybe you are the type of person who prefers to have fun on the drive to the office; similarly, your presentations can have entertainment while still being informative.

Once you know how to drive, you can do many things – you can go to the office; you can go on a date; you can go shopping; you can take your kids to school or take your parents on a surprise trip. Once you learn public speaking skills, you can speak with confidence: at your job, in your community, at a business presentation, at your school, on a variety of topics.

## 2. Fear strikes me whenever I want to give a presentation. What should I do?

To be honest, fear strikes everyone. Almost everybody gets nervous when they need to give a presentation. Trust me, even celebrities get nervous. In a presentation context, multiple people are focusing on what one person has to say. It seems threatening. Hence, we come across a feeling of fear.

Fear is an emotion that is hardwired into our bodies for the primary reason to ensure our safety. This fear response is the reason we experience physical changes like trembling, tenseness, rapid breathing, increased heart rate, sweating of palms and dry mouth brought about by fear of public speaking. In fact, many more weird things can be brought to the surface when faced with speaking in public and that includes phobia of public speaking.

A phobia is an excessive and unreasonable fear. Not sure which one you have? Let me help you find the answer through the following two scenarios.

Scenario One – The mere thought of the presentation makes you sweat, shiver and perspire. You are putting off preparing or even going to the venue to give the presentation. In this case, you might have more than plain fear. You might have a phobia. A very intense form of fear of public speaking is called glossophobia. If you feel this way, you need help to overcome it in the form of therapy. Yes, therapy does cost money, but without it you might not be able to pursue your dream of public speaking and, in the end, pay even a higher price. The following points will help you find the right therapist.

- Look for a therapist who excels in cognitive behavioral therapy and hypnotherapy.

- Check the success rate of the therapist in helping clients overcome glossophobia.

- Request a sample session so you can judge whether or not to hire this therapist to help you.

- Check to see if online or Skype sessions can be arranged if the therapist is not nearby.

Scenario Two – You have some level of anxiety but you still decide to go to the stage where you perspire, shake, shiver or lose your train of thought and then muddle through. In this case, the overwhelming emotion is only that of fear, nothing more.

Simple fear does not hinder you from presenting. *You got to the stage, faced the audience, spoke, yes, and maybe you fumbled,* but you still did it! Then, you are only suffering from simple fear and it can be overcome if you are willing to put out some effort. If you are, then I bet you are going to enjoy the ride. Are you ready?

You must start by accepting that the fear of public speaking is the fear of the unknown and fear of ridicule. To illustrate this point better, ask yourself the following questions:

- What will people think about me if I make mistakes during my presentation?

- Can I really sizzle on stage even though I don't have an eye-catching look?

- Am I worried that I won't give an effective presentation because English is not my first language?

- What exactly are the mechanics of speaking and how can I learn them?

- What happens if I go blank in the middle of a speech?

- What happens if the projector stops working?

- What are the chances of the PowerPoint crashing?

- What if an audience member asks a question and I don't know the answer?

Every one of the above questions relates to an aspect of unknown or ridicule. I'm sure you can think of even more, but these are the most common and will help you feel more comfortable on stage to overcome imagined ridicule.

Let us take a situation to find the specific questions that will fit your need.

Imagine a scenario where your boss says, "Tomorrow you are going to give a presentation about our project's performance to our senior management."

Put yourself in this situation. As you do this, think of any impeding questions and write them down on a piece of paper. These questions are your REAL FEARS.

Check out what you have written on that piece of paper and I am sure you will be able to find the answers to them as you read through the remainder of this book. Even if you do not find the exact question you have written down, if you read through to the end of this book, you'll probably learn enough to answer any questions about fear and make yourself confident enough to take the stage.

There is nothing like real knowledge and truth to overcome imagined fear.

## 3. What will other people think if I make a mistake during my presentation?

If this is something you have worried about, trust me, I did the same myself. Let me share something personal.

I bombed in my first public speaking attempt in front of the whole school. But in my case, rather than actually being embarrassed by the fear of forgetting my speech, I was scared of being ridiculed by my classmates. Even though it was a significant incident for me, nobody, I mean nobody ever ridiculed me for that performance.

There are two lessons that I learned from that experience. One, people respect you when you speak in front of an audience, and two, people only think about you, as much as you think they think of you.

I do not want to lie to you, but if your goal is to give flawless presentations, you first have to accept that you need to learn by making mistakes. Only practice makes perfect. Ask anybody who has achieved success in their chosen field and every one of them will tell you that they faced failure at some point in their life. But the point is that they succeeded beyond it.

Once you are seen as a presenter, your audience will respect you for being on stage. If you perform well, it is a bonus. If you end up giving a mediocre presentation, they won't even remember it, but you still get the benefit of that onstage experience.

Now, I will reveal two secrets to help you see dramatic changes in yourself as a speaker.

Secret number one – Speak as often as possible and at every given opportunity.

Secret number two – Take the time to reflect on every experience by asking what went right, what went wrong, and for suggestions on how to do it better next time. Later in the book, you will find specific action items and details to reflect on your experience. To illustrate this point better, let me use the iPhone 6 as an example. This particular model was not launched first, iPhone 1 had to be launched first. Then, reflecting on previous models, newer versions kept coming every year.

You will not start out by giving a perfect presentation, but if you reflect on your prior experience and keep at it, your presentations will evolve and eventually get better and better. So do not worry about what people will think of you, think about how you will learn from any mistakes in order to give a better presentation the next time.

## 4. Can I really sizzle on stage even though I don't have an eye-catching look?

By this statement, I mean good looks, good height or other traits provided by Mother Nature. We automatically judge people by how they look.

To be honest, we are being judged 24/7. Yes, people who have an eye-catching look might always have an undue advantage, but for the rest of us, we must hone our abilities and exude qualities such as enthusiasm, attitude, sincerity, word power, solid reasoning, emotion *and many more that can be acquired.* For example, Winston Churchill, Martin Luther King and Mahatma Gandhi were actually short men, but nevertheless, they went into the annals of history as powerful public speakers because of their acquired qualities.

Be inspired by these great speakers to look for and practice your strengths; maybe yours is a knack for comic timing; maybe your enthusiasm is contagious; maybe you have the natural ability to explain complex terms in a simple manner. Initially, you might not know your strength, however, once you find it – and it will come once you start speaking regularly – use it to your advantage.

## 5. Even though speaking comes naturally to me, do I still need to prepare my presentation?

Ok, so you were born with the gift of gab, many of us (me, included) do not have that gift. People think I do and say to me, "You got a gift."

I wish they knew how many boring hours have been spent writing, rewriting and rehearsing my presentations.

After studying champions, hearing world-class coaches, participating in competitive speaking, I understood that PREPARATION is the key to sizzle on stage.

If speaking comes naturally to you, then you are ahead of the game, but you will still have to prepare your speech for structure, clarity, message, call to action, etc.

The point – being a natural speaker is only one aspect (it is an advantage), but knowing how to be a prepared speaker is another aspect (it is an unfair advantage!). I always recommend being a prepared speaker. When you are prepared, you will come across as being natural (not fake) and people will believe you. There are two aspects to being prepared: Either you have sufficient time or you do not.

If you have sufficient time, then the best option is to have your speech committed to MUSCLE MEMORY. If your speech is in your muscle memory, it means that you don't have to focus on your next thought or word during the actual presentation. It works like a charm. However, it takes work and time. We'll discuss more about this in a later part of this book.

If you do not have sufficient time to commit your speech to muscle memory, you can use notes. You might have been told, "Do not use notes because you will lose credibility." And although that may be true in some circumstances, the statement can be misinterpreted. What it actually means is that using notes is OK as long as you DON'T READ verbatim from them or use them as a script. In fact, if you want proof that notes are fine when used correctly, just take a look at Steve Jobs in his famous "Stay Hungry, Stay Foolish" keynote speech at the 2005 Stanford graduation ceremony – he used notes!

Even if you know how to use notes properly, you will still need to prepare beforehand. Remember – there is *no replacement* for adequate preparation.

The following are specific situations where having notes can be really helpful.

- In a technical presentation, notes can anchor a presentation and keep it on track without getting lost in depths of one particular topic.

- In a persuasive talk, you can use notes to make sure you correctly recite a poem or quote.

- If your presentation is the keynote address for an event or session (especially for formal events/corporate events), notes can be very effective.

Do not assume that you need not prepare because you have notes. Even with notes, you have to be comfortable with your content and that means you need to rehearse your script. *Your words must smoothly roll off your tongue.* Repeating this important point once again: there is no replacement for rehearsal and preparation.

## 6. Can I still give an effective presentation even without a strong vocabulary?

I'll let you in on a secret. Even though English was my first language in school, my mother tongue is Telugu. Maybe you are hearing that name for the first time. Because you purchased this book, I am assuming you do not have a problem with English. But no matter what your language is, people all over the world have the same worry that they do not have a strong vocabulary. If you fall into this category and don't feel your vocabulary is strong enough, I have good news for you.

Oral communication is a much different ball game than written communication. I am going to prove this to you. While listening to a speaker, how many chances does the audience get to listen to that speech or presentation? Only one chance! So from the following two options, which one do you think is the most effective?

1. Vocabulary that an audience needs to search out its meaning in a dictionary.

2. Vocabulary comprised of common words that are easy to understand.

Option 2 is the obvious answer. Using simple words that we speak in day-to-day conversations is the key to a well-received presentation.

Consider this example. You could say, "Since its inception, our company has endeavored to be cognizant of the fact that employee proficiencies are important." Or you could say, "Since its start, our company has been aware that employee skills are important."

Even though the meanings of the above examples are similar, the second option was easy to understand.

Don't you agree?

In fact, I have seen campaigns in health insurance companies such as Aetna to persuade their employees to use simple words to communicate with their customers. Craig Valentine, the 1999 World Champion of Public Speaking, says, "When you are in speaking, you are in sales."

This drives home the point that if you are playing the role of a speaker, then your audience member is playing the role of a customer. Hence, use simple words to serve your audience.

Your audience will judge you based on the value of what you say, rather than the glamor of your individual words.

# CHAPTER 2.

# Speech Creation

In which you'll learn about purpose, structure and specific ideas to create speech elements such as an opening, context setting, key points, supporting points, etc.

## 7. I know my topic but I feel stuck. What am I missing?

Feeling stuck will *stop you from taking action*. It has happened to me. Based on my experience, I realize that we often miss a very important step when preparing presentations. This important step is finding and knowing the *purpose* of the presentation.

You can determine this based on the *objective, occasion* and *outcome*. For example, for an after-dinner speech or a best man's speech, your purpose should be to entertain. In the case of a business presentation to senior management to implement an idea, your purpose should be to persuade. Here the purpose relates to the style or approach that you'll take to accomplish the overall goal of your presentation.

The other reason for getting stuck could be because of not defining a core thesis for your talk. Have you ever experienced sitting through an entire presentation only to ask yourself once it's over, "What was that presentation about?" If your response to yourself is, "You know.... it was this thing... I am not really sure," that means that the presentation did not have a core thesis. A core thesis should be clear, short and add value to the audience. As a presenter, it is very important to determine this. And you can do so by knowing what you want your audience to feel, think or do after your presentation.

Let us imagine that you are a business analyst for a healthcare firm. One fine day, your boss asks you to give a talk about your business area to 50 new recruits. Let us say your business area is claims processing. In this case, what will be the purpose of your speech? Begin by asking and answering some general questions, such as: What is the objective? *Educate the new recruits*. What is the occasion? *A presentation to first-day recruits*. What is the outcome? *The recruits need to understand the business area*. Based on the answers cited above, you can determine that the overall purpose (or the style) "to inform" seems to be a good fit.

Regarding core thesis, we know it has to be short, clear and add value to the audience. It'll be the takeaway for your audience. To determine this, ask yourself: "What do I want the audience to think, feel or do differently after listening to my talk?" Considering the above data points, you can formulate something like, "Understanding claims processing will make your job easier."

Now, let us assume there is another important detail that needs to be addressed in the above scenario. A major project (let's call it X) is going to start the next day and all the new recruits in your area must start work on it immediately. In this case, you know even if they understand the claims processing business, their job will not be easy because they have to work on a major project with an immediate effect. So, in that case your overall purpose (or style) can be "to persuade" them. You can modify the core thesis to something like, "Working on project X will get you visibility from the CEO."

Note – Just because you decided your overall purpose (or style) is "to inform" does not mean you cannot be entertaining or persuasive. A real-time speech always has a mix of different types of styles, such as *entertaining and informing* or *entertaining and persuading*; however, one of these styles is always dominant.

Let us look at a case study. In order to make this easy, I'll refer to this same case study throughout the remainder of this book. This study is based on a speech I gave at an event while I was creating this book. The following is the high-level transcript of my invitation:

Phone rings.

*Me:* "Hello."

*Caller:* "Hi Rama. How are you?"

*Me:* "I am good."

*Caller:* "This is Tom <name changed>. I am the anchor for Jim's <name changed> 20th anniversary event. This event is to acknowledge the 20-year membership of Jim in our community. We were wondering if you could speak on this occasion?"

*Me:* "Sounds great. Can you please let me know the date of the event?"

*Caller:* "On the 15th of November."

*Me:* "That works for me. How long can I speak?"

*Caller:* "About 7 minutes."

*Me:* "Do you want me to speak on any particular topic?"

*Caller:* "About Jim. Your experiences... You know."

*Me:* "Hm. Sure. I can work on it."

*Caller:* "So, I'll send an email with time, venue and location. Please send your title and introduction within a couple of days."

*Me:* "Sure."

*Caller:* "Thank you, Rama."

*Me:* "My pleasure. See you soon."

Phone call ends – click.

Now, let us discuss some of the highlights of this interview (here, the *questions and answers* exchanged serve as the interview) and see what they tell you about the intended purpose of this speech.

From the conversation, it is evident that the meeting planner wants to showcase Jim for his 20-year tenure in the community. I've known Jim for almost 5 years. He is a bundle of energy. He has the ability to spread cheer while also being a sharp salesman. Based on the above data points, I felt an entertaining speech would suit the occasion. So, my overall purpose was "to entertain." Since the occasion was showcasing the 20-year stint of this person, my core thesis was "learn lessons from Jim." Ideally, the core thesis in an entertaining speech need not follow all the rules. However, the topic should be clear. In our case, the topic is Jim.

## 8. How do I start creating content for my presentation?

Any content you consume, whether it is a movie, article, newspaper, or this book – it has one thing in common and that is *structure*. Think about it, even when you are casually sharing something with your friends, talking about an experience, notice that structure is always present. And, as we all know, the most important function of structure is to add shape and support something, in this case – your presentation. The first step in creating content is determining a suitable structure in which you'll organize and present your content.

The following is a basic skeletal structure: an *opening, context setting, key points, support points, application, summary* and *conclusion*. For simplicity, key points, support points and application are listed in sequential order. However, they can be organized in any order.

- Opening
- Context Setting
  - Key point 1
  - Supporting point 1
  - (Application of point 1) – *Good to have*
  - Key point 2
  - Supporting point 2
  - (Application of point 2) – *Good to have*
- Summary
- Conclusion

Opening is what you say in the first 30 or 60 seconds.

Context setting is explaining what you are going to tell them. Sometimes, this part gets merged into your opening.

Key points help to reinforce the core thesis of your talk. A good rule of thumb is to have three or four key points in a talk.

Supporting points substantiate or prove a key point. You can use stories, statistics, illustration or facts for support. You can use one or more of these elements for support.

Application specifically tells the audience how to apply the key point.

Summary drives home what you have told them and recaps your presentation. Sometimes, it gets mingled with conclusion.

Conclusion is the showstopper for your presentation. This is the final 30 or 60 seconds of your presentation.

A word of caution about structure – even though you learnt a basic structure above, structure can be customized based on your needs. I would recommend you start with a basic skeletal structure. You can always tweak it as your presentation evolves.

For continuity purposes, let us take the example of our case study. I used the following structure for that presentation.

- Opening
- Context Setting
  - Story 1
  - Point 1
  - Story 2
  - Point 2
  - Illustration/story for point 2
  - Point 3
  - Facts for point 3

- Illustration/fact for point 3

- Summary

- Conclusion

Visit http://publicspeakking.com/37steps and download the ready-to-go speech templates. Speech creation will become much easier.

## 9. How do I create a killer opening for my talk?

We all want a killer opening for our presentations. Don't we?

Before I go into the specific strategies, you need to understand the purpose of the opening and how it impacts the rest of the speech.

Write this down. *The first 30 or 60 seconds of your presentation determines how well the rest of the presentation will go.*

The aim of the opening is to make sure the audience is going to listen to the whole presentation. An effective opening hooks your audience to listen to you. After your opening, if the individuals in your audience are whispering to each other or checking their phones, you know you had better create a better opening.

Let me walk you through some surefire openings guaranteed to get the audience's attention. Choose the one that suits your specific need.

**Four Keys for a Killer Opening:**

**1. Start With a Current Observation About Your Surroundings and the Occasion for Which You Are Speaking:** Being completely present and saying something relevant to the occasion is always a great opening. The following examples will give you some ideas.

If you received a flattering introduction, it is appropriate to use self-deprecating humor. By doing this, you will release tension. In fact, this works to make your audience start liking you. Example: "Thank you for that lovely introduction, I wish my dad was here. At least now, he would have felt proud of me."

If you are speaking in a foreign country, using a greeting in the native language is always a great opening. For example, you are an American and are speaking in India. Saying "Namaste" will create an instant connection with the audience. "Namaste" is a Hindi word and a traditional way to greet someone in India.

You can also mention the things that everybody is experiencing but nobody is talking about (the elephant in the room). Let us say the air conditioning is set too high and you find it uncomfortable. Most probably your audience feels the same. By acknowledging this, you grab their attention and remove the distraction from their mind. In this situation, you can say something like, "I usually stand tall, but right now, I am feeling too cold to talk to you. I am freezing." You might get a laugh as well (and that is always good).

**2. Start With a Question:** Asking a question engages the audience, stops them in their tracks and guides them to think in one direction. The question could be rhetorical (where you don't expect an answer) or reciprocal (where you expect an answer). For example, if you are doing a business presentation on knowledge management, you could ask a reciprocal question, "What is the most important aspect of knowledge management?" If only a few people respond, cheerfully involve more people by prompting. "Sir, what do you think?" Now, others have their antenna up because you might call on them next. Now, you have your audience thinking in one direction.

**3. Start With a Startling Statistic:** You can start off with a startling statistic related to your topic. For example, Jamie Oliver started his TED talk (Teach every child about food) with a statistic regarding food, "Sadly, in the next 18 minutes when I do our chat, four Americans that are alive will be dead from the food that they eat." This one is a chilling statistic. It is not entertaining but chilling. Still, it is a killer opener because it got their attention.

**4. Start With a Personal Story or Experience:** Story is a simple yet powerful way to start your talk. There is no better strategy to capture the attention of the audience and get them interested in listening to the rest of your talk. For example, in our case study, I used the following. "I know Jim since 2009. At that time, he was a big man. Even now he is a big man, physically. To describe Jim in one line – Jim is like a 120-liter Coca-Cola bottle opening happiness everywhere he goes. That's it. I am done."

Let us look at another example. Susan Cain, author of *Quiet*, started her TED talk (*The power of introverts*) with a beautiful story about her childhood, "When I was nine years old I went off to summer camp for the first time. And my mother packed me a suitcase full of books, which to me seemed like a perfectly natural thing to do because in my family, reading was the primary group activity. And this might sound antisocial to you, but for us it was really just a different way of being social. You have the animal warmth of your family sitting right next to you, but you are also free to go roaming around the adventure land inside your own mind."

Specific Strategies for an Effective Opening:

- Take a few seconds to scan your audience before uttering the opening words. By doing this, you are capturing their attention even before you start speaking.

- Do not start with fillers such as "The weather is good," "What a sunny day," etc. You can say "good morning" or "good afternoon" but you can say this after getting their proper attention by using the strategies listed above.

- Build trust. Be open to your audience. By using open palms, a gentle smile and resonant voice, you will open up and start building trust. Try to avoid high-pitched, exaggerated movements in your opening. Your audience might lose trust if you overdo things.

- Listen to your audience. If you greet them with "good morning," the audience might greet you back. If you are truly listening, you should acknowledge the greeting by smiling or gesturing.

- Be relaxed and comfortable. In most scenarios, your audience wants you to do well on stage. By being relaxed and comfortable, you are telling them that you are doing well.

- Make them like you. You can do this by not showing a know-it-all attitude.

- Tone down the entertainment factor for a business presentation. Starting with an observation or question is a safe bet.

## 10. What is a context setting and how do I create one?

This is a very important step in any presentation and one that is often missed.

To put it in simple words – it is telling your audience about what you are going to tell them. It could either be a promise that you will eventually fulfill or a problem that you can solve during your speech.

<u>Specific Steps to Set a Compelling Context:</u>

1. Context should be audience focused. The audience should feel it is about them. How about saying this, "After listening to my talk, you will walk away with specific ideas on how you can achieve your goals." Don't, for example, say, "Today, I am going to tell you how I achieved all my goals" because it is not audience focused.

2. Context should be clear and specific. Your audience should be able to clearly understand your agenda. For example, after adding the clarity factor to the above statement, it reads, "After listening to my talk, you will walk away with specific ideas on how you can achieve your goals for this year."

3. Go even further and add a specificity factor along the lines of, "After my talk, you will walk away with three turnkey principles that will help you achieve your 1-year-goals."

By combining the three steps of audience focus, clarity and specificity, you can finally say, "After my talk, you will walk away with three turnkey principles that will help you achieve your 1-year goals."

The more you think and rewrite, the better you will set your context.

## 11. How do I select the key points for my presentation?

Selecting key points for your presentation is another turnkey activity. If you want to sizzle and set yourself apart from the rest, you have to select *relevant* key points that suit core thesis *of your speech.* When you give a talk, there is always an entity or person who is responsible for running that event.

The following strategies will help you select relevant key points for your presentation.

**Interview**: Interview is the best way to create key points. If you have access to your audience before the actual presentation, you can interview a few of them to understand their key problems or requirements. Based on the responses, you can frame your key points. However, the simplest and quickest way to frame content is by interviewing the presentation planner. An interview with the presentation planner not only gives you an idea about the purpose of your talk but also gives you an idea about the key points of your talk.

Let us take an example at your job. Imagine your boss tells you to talk to your team about a recent organizational change. What will be your first step? As we have discussed earlier, you should be using the interview strategy. You have to understand that your boss is functioning as your presentation planner. Interview him or her. In this case, occasion and objective are pretty clear; hence ask him or her, "What is the desired outcome of this presentation?" "What are the three or four major points that need to be communicated?" "Is there any adverse impact to the team?" The answers to these questions will give you enough points so that you can take the best ones to create *relevant* key points.

Now, let us take our main case study. I had given a snapshot of the short telephone interview. In this case, I could not get detailed information. In fact, the presentation planner just told me to talk about Jim. I had to do some analysis and come up with key points. Let me take you through the process. The occasion was to acknowledge the 20-year tenure of Jim in the community. The objective was to showcase the benefits of the community program. The outcome was to empower new members in the community. To find the key points, I had to start from the core thesis – learn lessons from Jim. When I took some time and thought about Jim, the three things that came to my mind were "solid support," "selling skills" and "passionate attitude." These are great points. Since our core thesis is to "learn lessons from Jim," I thought it would be a great idea to convey these points as lessons we can learn from Jim, but how could I frame the lessons? This is where *audience analysis* comes into play.

**Audience Analysis**: In order to do audience analysis, answer the following questions:

- What are the common experiences among the audience?

- What kind of experiences do you and the audience have in common?

- What kind of problems can you solve for the audience through your presentation?

- How can you genuinely help the audience learn something new to improve their life?

- How can you help the audience do the things they know that they should be doing but are currently not doing?

After answering the above questions, try to combine the answers from your experience, the data from the interview and audience analysis.

In our case study, more than 90 percent were paid members of the community. Helping each other is the heartbeat of the community. So I connected my first perception (solid support) of Jim and the idea of helping each other, to form my first lesson, "Give solid support to someone in need." Even though the community was a non-profit organization, members need to pay a minimal membership fee. So it involves selling. As a general rule, selling has a bad rap. I wanted to change that mindset. So I connected my second perception (selling skills) of Jim and the idea of changing their mindset, to form my second lesson, "Selling is not hard." Being passionate in whatever we do gives us great results. You know it. I know it. Everyone knows it, but we forget it. So I connected my third perception (passionate attitude) of Jim and the idea that people forget to be passionate, to form my third lesson, "Be passionate in what you do." So I framed the key points: "Give solid support to someone in need," "Selling is not hard," "Be passionate in what you do." I wanted the audience to use these lessons in their journey as well as in their life. So I selected the supporting stories, facts and illustration related to experiences around the community so that the audience could relate.

To summarize, in order to select key points, you first need to understand the objectives and occasion of the presentation. This will help you clarify your purpose as well as provide fodder for your key points. Once you are clear on your purpose, use your interview and/or audience analysis to form what will be your relevant key points.

## 12. How do I support the key points of my presentation?

Before we get into the details on how to use supporting points, you first need to understand the solid concepts of public speaking based on Aristotle's perspective. Aristotle was a great philosopher and orator. He was awesome. In fact, some consider his teachings as the basis of modern Western civilization. Aristotle, in his masterpiece *Rhetoric*, says that an effective speech has three key elements, which I have explained below:

1. Ethos

2. Logos

3. Pathos

*Ethos* refers to the credibility of the speaker. It should answer why YOU should speak on the particular occasion. This is your qualifications, achievements, etc. Forget about public speaking, even in one-on-one communication, someone will listen to you only when they find you credible. It is imperative that you be trustworthy and likeable. For any talk, you'll have to be high on ethos factor. If you are already an expert, and you are called to speak on the topic, then you have an advantage. You don't need to go out of the way to build trust. However, your words and speech should mirror this perception. On the other hand, if many do not know you, then you have got to prove that you are the right person to give the presentation.

*Logos* refers to the reasoning behind the point. In practical sense, this is the logic behind the point. Logical appeal makes the audience *think*. You might be doing this currently (use of statistics, facts, illustrations) but now you know why you are doing it! For instance, if the key point is "Work smarter, not harder," the supporting point can be, "A researcher from MIT says that if we do an early morning walk for 15 minutes, our productivity increases 3 times."

*Pathos* is the emotional attachment between the speaker and the audience. In general, most of the decisions in life are controlled by emotion rather than logic. So, as a speaker, if you can tap into that emotional need of your audience, you can make them *act*. And that's precisely why stories are so powerful. For example, say your key point is "Work smarter, not harder." You can support it by telling a story like "During my 6th grade summer vacation, I remember feeling uncomfortable getting up early in the morning to go for a walk. But my dad compelled me. When I started walking on the green grass, holding his hand, looking at the clear blue sky in that pleasant weather, I just loved the whole experience. After a few days, I started looking forward to it. It soon became a habit and I have followed the habit of an early morning walk to date. After the walk, every morning I feel so energetic and full of life that I finish my tasks in the first 4 hours at my office. My life would have never been the same if I had not followed that habit till today." How was the story? Do you feel like taking a walk? That's the power of pathos.

The use of logos and pathos will vary based on your need. In fact, I would say if you want your audience to think differently, be high on logos. If you want your audience to feel or act differently, be high on pathos. Practically, a presentation will have all three elements (ethos, logos, pathos) with different percentages. Remember, depending on your need, the supporting points come in different sizes and shapes. If you want to persuade your audience to create good habits, your entire speech can be made of one single story or multiple stories or a mix of stories, statistics, facts or stories mixed with facts. It is an amazing experience to design a presentation. I used the word "design" because your content is like a product and it has to be designed so that it can function well.

Now that you understand ethos, logos and pathos, I can talk about using supporting points. In the skeletal structure, you saw *Point followed by support* and vice versa. This is the place where you need to figure out how to support your key point, but first you'll need to understand the four widely used elements for creating support: stories, statistics, facts and illustration.

**Stories**: Carmine Gallo, in his bestselling book Talk Like TED, says, "Tell stories to reach people's hearts and minds." Story is an age-old way to keep your presentation interesting. Stories are really powerful because they can emotionally connect you to your audiences. In short, stories help you in emotional arguments. We'll talk more about story in the coming sections. For now, let us see how I used story in our case study. This is the first story in the case study speech.

> In 2009, a contest was in progress. Jim was the host. He asked the facilitator to close the door and stand out guarding the room. One empathetic audience member shouted, "'Mr. Jim, he will miss the contest. This is not fair." In such a tense situation, what would you reply? I would have said, "Yes. Let me ask him to stand inside so that he can also see the contest" or something to support the cry. But Jim said those unforgettable words – "Yes, yes, he will miss the contest." Our audience member went speechless. No further comments.

> Later in the year, I competed in my first humorous speech contest. Somehow, I crossed the 3rd level of contest. People were saying things like "you did not win because you were funny. You won because others were less funny." I wanted help. I reached out to many and finally Jim gave me a hug and said, "I will help you." He arranged for a mentoring session for one full day at my home. That day, Jim and a few others came to my home. You know what was the first question he asked, "What do we have for lunch?" I was like, "Really?" But the inputs and ideas that were discussed that day helped me cross the semifinals and be among the final 6 speakers in the entire district. The lesson: give solid support to someone in need.

Generally, anecdotes are also used in presentations. Anecdotes are nothing but amusing stories, which are short, personal and to the point. I had used the following anecdote in my case study speech.

Mr. Jim has mastered the art of closing the sale. He asks three questions.

"Did you like the meeting?"

"Yes."

"Would you like to be a member?"

"Yes."

"Is there anything stopping you from becoming a member?"

"Um... I do not have cash."

"I'll accompany you to the ATM machine."

How easy was that? The lesson – selling is not hard.

**Statistics**: Statistics are only the use of data to prove a point. Statistics always help you win a logical argument. Statistics are powerful because they act as proof. However, you'll have to make sure that you relate the statistic to your audience.

For example, you need to say more than, "1 billion people are affected by mood swings." Instead, say something like, "In 2014, the FDA reported that 1 billion people are affected by mood swings. This means one in 7 people in this room are affected by mood swings."

Let me give another instance. In his famous TED talk (<u>Teach every child about food</u>), Jamie Oliver says, "We need a revolution. Mexico, Australia, Germany, India, China, all have massive problems of obesity and bad health. Think about smoking. It costs way less than obesity now. Obesity costs you Americans 10 percent of your healthcare bills, 150 billion dollars a year. In 10 years, it's set to double: 300 billion dollars a year. And let's be honest, guys, you ain't got that cash."

Imagine how effective it is to say that healthcare cost for obesity is going to be 300 billion dollars in the next 10 years rather than just saying that obesity is going to increase healthcare cost.

Dos and Don'ts for Correctly Using Statistics:

- Don't present too much data at once. It will confuse your audience.

- Do some simple math to do the analysis and present the data so the data will make sense.

- Do quote the relevant source of the data, be it your own research or that of a well-known entity.

**Facts:** Facts are things that are true and that everyone accepts as true. These could be findings from an experiment, an article in a newspaper or public information that everybody agrees upon. Facts can be really useful when you start off on the same note, where both you and the audience agree upon something. Then, you can state your key point to a receptive audience.

Now for example, in our case study, my third key point was "Be passionate in what you do." Let us see how it went. I started off by stating the fact that "3 years ago our city had only 8 to 10 clubs. Now, our city has more than 25 clubs because of his leadership." I said this to emphasize his passion for the community and the results he could achieve by being passionate. This supported my key point, "Be passionate in what you do."

**Illustration:** Illustration is showing the audience your content in a simple yet creative way. You can illustrate your point using PowerPoint, props, a writing board, flip charts or a combination of facts and questions. Let me explain one by one.

<u>PowerPoint:</u> If you are in the corporate world, I think you surely agree that hardly any presentation happens without a PowerPoint. We are in an age where PowerPoint has become a synonym for presentation. But, today you are going to learn the truth. Now remember this phrase: PowerPoint is only the tool. It is not the presentation. First assess if you really need PowerPoint slides. If you feel the need, only then go ahead and use it. When used correctly, PowerPoint can be a really good medium. You can utilize pictures, flow charts or diagrams to support your point. Let me give an example of how a PowerPoint illustration can increase the effectiveness of a presentation. There was a contest to solve parking problems in our corporate office. Out of the many entries, only a few could move on to the next round. The ones that did move on were smart enough to take a snapshot of the campus using Google maps and showed us open space that could be used for additional parking. They showed us the solution – that's Illustration. In a nutshell, the ones who moved on were able to illustrate their solution better than others.

Dos and Don'ts for Using PowerPoint:

1. Do plan the complete order of your slides. Brainstorm the whole flow on a white board or paper Instead of opening the tool in your computer.

2. Do create PowerPoint slides using the following rules. These rules have been designed keeping a traditional outlook. However, if you want to design unique and captivating slides, I would recommend you check out <u>How to Design TED Worthy Presentation Slides</u> by Akash Karia. It is a great step-by-step resource in which Akash has analyzed presentation slides given at TED and presented the information in a user-friendly format. Now, let us learn the rules.

- Do use the minimum number of slides.

- Don't write more than 6 words per each bullet point.

- Do make all words clear and legible.

- Don't have more than 3 or 4 bullet points in a slide. If you really want to sizzle, use only one point per slide accompanied by a suitable illustration.

- Do create and use blank slides (full black) between the actual presentation slides to act as a transition mechanism from focusing on the slide to focusing on you.

3.  Do rehearse the coordination between the slide transition and your delivery.

4.  Do prepare so you'll be able to speak even if you don't have the PowerPoint slides.

5.  Don't ever turn your back to your audience to look at the slides and explain what is pictured. You have to know what is given in the slide. You should be the focus.

6.  Do instruct the person controlling the PowerPoint to move on to the blank slide if the slide is not relevant. If you do not have a blank slide, temporarily turn off the presentation by pressing B in your computer or laptop keyboard. Alternatively, you can buy a remote control to navigate between slides or turn off your presentation.

Properties (Props): These are nothing but physical objects used for illustrating a point. Props have significant impact when used in an appropriate manner. Let me give an example. A speaker was talking about work-life balance. He just started off saying the things he did from morning till night on a Monday. He repeated the same things for Tuesday. Now, the audience started laughing. The audience got the point that we are highly caught up in the mundane things of life. Then, the speaker took a balloon and started blowing it up. The more he blew, the more uncomfortable we got. And then, finally the balloon burst. I was in the audience and could feel the impact of the point he was trying to make. He didn't even state his key point, but we still got it. That's the power of a good prop.

Dos and Don'ts for Correctly Using Props:

- Don't use too many props or you will shift the audience's focus away from yourself.

- Don't keep the prop in audience view. Once the prop is used, hide it so that focus comes back to you.

- Do use a prop only when it is needed so it comes as a surprise element.

Writing board: This is another widely used device we have seen since childhood. I am referring to our classroom in school. The teachers used a board to draw a diagram or solve a problem which essentially illustrated their point. Even in the corporate world, we use boards/flip charts. These devices are suitable when you are co-creating something with the audience. In fact, in a famous TED talk (*How great leaders inspire action*), Simon Sinek used a board to explain the golden circle and why asking WHY is important.

To cite a personal example, I remember using the boards during membership sessions for people to join our corporate public speaking forum. I would look at everyone present in the room and ask, "What are you looking for?" I would hear, "Communication skills," "Event management skills," "Networking," "Overcoming fear," "Confidence," etc. I would write all the answers on the board using a marker. I would then explain how our corporate forum would fill their need. Since everything was written down on the board, the audience clearly understood what they were going to get. A flip chart does the same thing, but instead of a writing board, charts are pinned to a stand.

Questions and Facts: We can also illustrate our points by using a combination of questions and facts. For example, our case study made a point that Jim was passionate in what he did. I supported it with an illustration. I knew Jim loved visiting other countries. I knew for a fact that people also love visiting different countries. But I needed to show that Jim had traveled to more countries than the rest of the folks in the audience, to prove Jim's passion for traveling.

I asked, "How many of you have traveled to more than 1 country?" <15 hands went up>

"How many of you have traveled to more than 2 countries?" <10 hands went up>

"How many of you have traveled to more than 5 countries?" <2 hands went up>

"How many of you have traveled to more than 20 countries?" <None except one hand, who was a sailor>

Then I said, "Mr. Jim has traveled to more than 40 countries". This illustrated the point that Jim is passionate about traveling. Using a fact about his passion for the community and the illustration about his love for travel, I was able to support my key point, "Be passionate in what you do."

*Final thoughts:* It's important to remember that supporting content prepared for one type of audience will not necessarily hold good for another audience. For example, based on the case study, if Jim had also been part of another paid community and I was asked to speak in honor of his 20th year of membership, I would not have given the same presentation. However, if the key points applied to that community as well, I would keep them but would change the supporting points. I would use stories; facts and illustration of Jim's experience in that other community.

In fact, even when you speak to similar audiences but in different countries, you might still need to customize your content, just as driving is different in various parts of the world. In the United States, you drive on the right side of the road whereas in India you drive on the left side of the road. Similarly, creating content for public speaking also differs. You should create content based on culture, values, beliefs, etc. For example, if you are talking about leadership, you will connect more with your audience in the United States if you use stories of Martin Luther King or Steve Jobs whereas you will connect better with your audience in India if you relate stories about Mahatma Gandhi or Dhirubhai Ambani.

## 13. How to create a compelling story?

Storytelling is a powerful medium that when used correctly can create an emotional connect with your audience. First of all, you need to make sure that your story is compelling and not boring! Even big brands use stories to create advertisements. But if you do not know how to tell a compelling story, you will end up boring the audience.

Stories have the ability to transfer emotions. As human beings, we tend to be persuaded when emotion has a major role to play. Why do we cry when Jack dies at the end of the movie *Titanic*? We know Leonardo DiCaprio (who played the role of Jack) did not die. After all, someone has faked it. That's the power of a story – the ability to transfer the emotion.

Here are the simple yet powerful elements that'll help you craft a compelling story.

**Must-have elements in a story:**

- Conflict.

- A character with a desire (hero or heroine).

- Obstacles in that path.

- Overcoming obstacles.

- The point.

**Good-to-have elements in a story:**

- Event setting – The time and place of the story.

- Character building – What the characters look like, their vulnerabilities, etc.

- Dialogue – What the characters say to each other.

- Humor – Even though it is optional, humor makes a story more compelling.

- Emotion – Knowing what the characters are feeling can make the difference between a good story and a great story.

- Sensory words – Using words that evoke the senses of touch, sound, smell, vision or taste.

**An example of a non-boring story:**

I remember in my 9th grade, my classmate Vivek was unbeatable. I could never beat his rank in exams. Vivek had a big face, a thick voice and a lot of cholesterol. That day – we got our results for our midterm exams. Vivek got 5th rank and I got 15th. Not surprising but depressing. I worried that my classmates would think I was dumb – which I am not. We guys started discussing our ranks and Vivek said, "I wonder how these guys end up in the top three ranks." I said, "Vivek, even you can be in the top three if you study harder." And he goes, "You can't even beat my rank. Just shut your mouth and leave." But in front of everyone, I was humiliated. I was furious.

I went to my best buddy Rakesh and said, "I want to beat his rank. What do I do?"

He said, "Forget it."

"No."

He said, "Okay. I have an idea. Why don't you study every day? You will become better. You can even beat his rank."

I went home that evening. My friends called me to play. I said, "No." My sisters called me to watch television. I said, "No." My mom called me to eat noodles. I said, "Yes." After eating, I picked up my book to study. I studied and studied and studied until I fell asleep after 5 minutes. I started to sleep but I could not continue to sleep. That humiliation became my nightmare. Throwing away the soft cotton blanket, I woke up and cried, again and again. I studied so that I could stop crying. And I studied every single day. After few months, exams came. Then the results came and guess what? Vivek got the 6th rank and I got the 2nd rank in my class. My teacher was shocked. Vivek was shocked. I was shocked. It was like magic.

Fast-forward 14 years, if you were sitting with me in that coffee shop, you would have seen my best buddy Rakesh and me sipping freshly brewed cappuccino and recalling that school incident. Rakesh said, "Do you know the exact reason for your magic at school?" I said, "Hard work." He goes, "No, it's because of your habit of studying every single day. Habits create magic."

**Citing the must-have and good-to-have elements in the above story:**

Conflict – "'You can't even beat my rank. Just shut your mouth and leave."

Character with a desire – "I went to my best buddy Rakesh and said 'I want to beat his rank. What do I do?'"

Obstacles – "'Forget it,'" "to play," "to watch television," "to eat noodles," "I fell asleep."

Overcoming obstacles – "I studied so that I could stop crying. And I studied every single day."

Point – "Habits create magic."

Event setting – "My 9th grade."

Character building – For supporting character, "Vivek had a big face, a thick voice and a lot of cholesterol." For main character, this sentence, "I could never beat his rank in exams," was added to show vulnerability of the character.

Dialogues – Between Vivek and me, Rakesh and me.

Humor – It has been sprinkled along with every other element. The jabs were "a lot of cholesterol," "classmates would think I am dumb – which I am not," "He said, 'Forget it,'" "Vivek was shocked, my teacher was shocked, I was shocked." (This is also an example of the Rule of Three, which we will discuss in #17.)

Emotion – "But in front of everyone, I was humiliated," "I woke up and cried, again and again."

Sensory words – Soft cotton blanket.

## 14. How do I best use transitions in my speech?

Transitions maintain a smooth and clear flow between the opening, context setting, key points, supporting points, summary and conclusion. If a speech is like a journey, then transitions are the signboards. Imagine your audience going on a journey from Boston to Washington, D.C. Suppose there are no signboards on the freeway (no GPS as well!), your audience might be feeling lost and say, "Did we cross New York?" Similarly, if you do not have transitions in your speech, your audience might feel lost.

Transitions can be:

1. Verbal

2. Non-verbal

3. A combination of verbal and non-verbal

**Verbal:** Verbal transitions are words or phrases that are used for smooth flow of your ideas. The verbal transition acts as a bridge between the points you shared and the points yet to be shared. Different type of words or phrases can be used depending on the function of the transition. Let me explain the role of verbal transitions in the following places.

Context Setting: *Greeting the audience* is a good technique to connect opening to context setting. For example, "I know Jim since 2009. At that time, he was a big man. Even now he is a big man, physically. (*Audience laughs.*) To describe Jim in one line – Jim is like a 120-liter Coca-Cola bottle opening happiness wherever he goes. That's it. I am done. (*Audience laughs.*) Good evening, ladies and gentlemen, today you are going to walk away with three lessons I learnt from Jim." "Good evening, ladies and gentlemen" is the transition in this example.

Key Points: The following are some techniques to transition between your key points.

- Listed Transitions. If your key points are clear but unrelated to each other, then you can use listed transition.

  "The first lesson I learnt…

  "The second lesson I learnt…

  "The third lesson I learnt…"

- Callback transitions. A callback is nothing but repetition of words or sentences that were used earlier in the speech. The callback works as a great transition in the case of stories. By using callback, you anchor your speech to a set of words or sentences.

  "I have a dream" by Martin Luther King Jr. and "Yes, we can" by Barack Obama functioned as a callback. However, they also functioned as repeatable phrases.

- Acronym transitions. An acronym is a device where only the first letters of each word in a title or sentence are used to form another recognizable word. Acronyms are another classy transition tool. A wonderful example is the speech given by Nitin Gupta at the 2012 graduation of the University of Pennsylvania. He used an acronym called WALK where his key points were built on expansion of WALK (Witness, Accept, Love and Know Thyself). It is a beautiful speech for which he received a standing ovation.

Supporting Points: To connect supporting points to your key points, you can use supporting transitions such as "For instance," "Let me prove this to you" or "Let me explain."

Internal Transitions: Sometimes, in order to clarify your stand, you may want to use counter-argument statements. In that case, you can use "But," "However," or "In spite of."

If you are using more than one supporting point to strengthen your key point, you can use transitions such as "Moreover," "In addition to," or "And also."

For Summary: Here you can use "In summary," "As I wrap up," "As I said earlier, we saw…" "Today, we learnt…"

For Conclusion: The following are some useful transitions for conclusion. "If you do not remember anything which I said…" "I would like to end my…." "After you walk out…" "As I said in the beginning…" "I wish you…" "Thank you for being…"

**Non-Verbal:** Non-verbal transitions are visual transitions that help in the clarity of your speech. The following tools are highly recommended:

1. Movement

2. Pause

3. Prompted gestures

Even though we cover non-verbal aspects from a mechanics stand-point in a future section, I would like to state it here so you get the big picture on their use as transitions.

Movement: I have observed that movement can be used to transition from one point to another. For instance, you can move from one point on the stage to another point to show that you have moved from one city to another city.

In another instance, a speaker spoke from one area on the stage and talked about how men think, then, by moving to another area of the stage, he transitioned to how women think.

Pause: A deliberate long pause can work as a great transition tool. While you pause, the audience knows you are giving them time to think. Then, you can start talking about the next point. In fact, you can couple pause with movement for an effective transition.

Prompted Gestures: They are gestures to indicate transition. For example, you can indicate 1, 2 and 3 by holding up the correct number of fingers to transition between key points.

**A Combination of Verbal and Non-Verbal**: I want to say that transitions work best when verbal and non-verbal are combined. For example, the listed transitions work great when you say the list number verbally and prompt the list number using gestures – indicating *first* by using forefinger, indicating *second* by using both forefinger and middle finger and indicating *third* lesson by using fore, middle and ring finger.

*Final thoughts:* The above strategies work well. However, you can mix and match the above techniques or come up with something unique. Ask one question when you create the transition: "Are the signboards clear in the journey of your audience?"

## 15. How can I have an effective summary?

The summary conveys the idea that it is time to wrap up neatly and go home satisfied. A simple model to summarize would be something as follows, "So, as we have seen today... *<key point 1>*, *<key point 2>* ... *<last key point>*."

In our case study presentation, the summary was, "Today, I want you to walk away with the three lessons that I learnt from Jim. They are – give support to the ones who need it, selling is not hard, be passionate in what you do."

Depending on the need, you can have a Q&A session (questions and answers) during summary. Suppose you are giving a business presentation, usually there would be a need for Q&A. You can start off by saying, "What questions can I answer for you?" This encourages questions and is a more effective and professional way than saying, "Do you have any questions?"

Dos and Don'ts for an Effective Q&A:

- Do take a pause and answer straight to the point. Please do not beat around the bush.

- Do clarify any question that is not clear. Reiterate the question to the questioner. This will bring clarity to you and the audience.

- Do confirm your answer to all questions by saying, "Does that make sense?" Or "Does that answer your question?"

- Do act confident. You might not know all the answers but acting confident and saying, "I can find more information and get back" will be much appreciated.

- Don't try to be a know-it-all. An audience will easily figure out if you are trying to be correct when you clearly don't know the answer. If you are not sure, say that you are not sure. But if it is a genuine question, you can say that you'll get back offline and provide the answer (*and do get back*).

## 16. How do I create a memorable conclusion for my speech?

Your conclusion is your last chance to leave your audience on a high. In fact, the success of your presentation might depend on how well you end it. Probably, this is something your audience will remember for years. The following are some ideas for creating a memorable conclusion.

**Seven Ideas to Create a Memorable Conclusion:**

**1. Best Wishes Close:** You can wish someone best of luck or bless him or her at the end of your speech. In our case study presentation, the conclusion was: "I congratulate Jim on completing his 20-year tenure in our community and wish him all the best for the next 20 years."

**2. Gratitude Close:** You can thank the people who helped you reach where you are if you are talking about your story. Or, you can thank the audience for listening to you. For example, Lance Miller in his 2005

World Championship speech concluded by saying: "You have been a great audience."

**3. Answer Close:** If your speech has a question at the opening or context setting, your conclusion should answer the question to reinforce the point. In one of my speeches, I use the following for setting the context: "Do you remember anything unbeatable?" I concluded with the following as an answer: "You can beat the unbeatable using habits because habits create magic."

**4. Action Close:** You can prompt the audience to take action on your core message. You can use this option for an informative or persuasive presentation. Now for example, if you want to give a business presentation about goals for the next year, your conclusion could be something like: "You have heard what we are planning to do, I know we have done it in the past, I am sure if we work together, we can do it for the upcoming year."

**5. Dialogue Close:** You can use this option for a persuasive presentation. If your content is designed in such a way that a character in your story says a dialogue that reflects your core thesis or message, you can use the same dialogue to conclude your presentation. For example, you use the following in your speech: "When I sat crying in the corner of my home for not scoring well in exams, my mom would come near me and say, 'Come on, you should be adamant till you get what you want.'" You can conclude by saying something like, "If my mom would have been here, she would say, 'Come on, you should be adamant till you get what you want.'"

**6. Poem Close:** You can use a poem to conclude your presentation. I think you should use this in an inspiring or persuasive presentation. Sir Ken Robinson in his famous TED talk (*Bring on the learning revolution*) read a short poem from W.B. Yeats about dreams. It was an inspiring talk and the poem that he read as the conclusion was the icing on the cake.

**7. Circular Close:** Circular close is one of the best techniques to close a presentation. The idea is to bring your audience back to the starting point, before you end. To give you a perspective from the movie world, *Titanic* is a classic example of the circular close. The opening of the movie showed Rose was an old lady. Then, the core content of the movie showed the love story of young Rose and in the closing, we again see old Rose as she reminisces about Jack and drops the necklace in the ocean. Let us take an informative speech example to understand this technique in a speech setting. I was coaching my friend for his speech on "Six Thinking Hats." For this presentation, his opening was "Who can tell me one common thing we encounter every day? It is a problem." In the body, we designed the content by illustrating the six thinking hats technique using stories. For the conclusion, we used a circular close: "So, the next time you encounter the common thing called problem – remember six thinking hats."

If you had an eagle eye, you would have noticed use of another technique in the above example. Yes, it is the answer close. What it proves is that there is no limit to the applications of the techniques and strategies shown above. The more creative you get, the more memorable your conclusion will get.

## 17. How do I refine my speech content?

Even though we prepared the content, unless we refine, it won't shine. While being coached for a contest, Jerry, my mentor said something remarkable. He said, "You win in speaking by writing." I could not agree more. I will not go into the nitty-gritty of presentation refinement, however, by using the following tools you will have a classy content.

**Four Tools to Refine Your Content:**

**1. Choose Simple Words With the Fewest Syllables:** Simple words mean everyday words that are used in regular communication. Anyone hearing the sentence should get the meaning instantly. A quick rule of thumb: "If someone is going to take more than a second to think about the meaning of any word, then chuck that word out." Using words with few syllables makes it easier for the listener. You can achieve this by taking a look at the script and replacing long or complicated words with their simpler and shorter synonyms. A combination of simple words and those without many syllables is powerful if you aim to be understood and not misunderstood. For example, instead of using "discernible" use "visible," or instead of using "obnoxious" use "mean."

**2. Use Active Voice:** Active voice is easy to follow. Our hearing is tuned to listen to active voice. Example: The meaning of the sentence "Jim hit Jack" will register faster than its passive voice "Jack was hit by Jim."

**3. Repeat Key Phrases:** This is the key to a classy speech. If you have seen Obama's presidential acceptance speech, notice that he used "Yes, we can" as his key phrase. King created a revolution with "I have a dream" as the key phrase in his speech. These speeches went into the annals of history because the key phrases were memorable. While creating an inspiring or persuasive speech *repeat the key phrases* to set you apart from the crowd.

**4. Use Rhetorical Devices:** These are tools to simplify the meaning and make it easy for your listener to understand your point. The most common uses of rhetorical devices are in the form of:

Similes: Comparing a lesser-known concept to a common concept with the use of word "like" or "as." The beauty of simile is that we can explain an unknown entity with the help of a well-known entity. This adds variety, spice and clarity to your speech. In our case study, we used "Jim is like a 120-liter Coca-Cola bottle, opening happiness wherever he goes." The audience got an idea about Jim in one sentence. They understood that Jim is cheerful, Jim is energetic and Jim is fat.

If you chuckled, you learnt a powerful technique to create humor. It is the *rule of three* in action. The formula is that the first two items are related and the third one is unrelated: "cheerful" and "energetic" are related whereas "fat" is unrelated.

Metaphors: A big brother to the simile. Here, instead of comparing, we refer a concept or a person to another entity. Metaphors not only add spice and decoration to your speech, but also bring depth of the meaning we want to convey. It helps the listeners to understand the concept better because they know the characteristics of the entity to which you are referring. For example: When audiences hear "Jim, you are great," they might wonder, "How great is Jim?" Instead, if they hear, "Jim, you are a rock star" (rock star is the metaphor), the audience is associating the characteristics of a rock star to Jim.

Alliterations: These are words with similar sounding syllables that have a pleasing effect on the listener. This is very powerful. Let me show you why. Follow the italicized syllables. "*Men* Are from *Mars* and *Women* Are from *Venus*." This title is catchy because the M sound and V sound create the magic. Why are terms such as "bad boy" and "good girl" used quite often? The B sound and G sound create a pleasing effect for the listener. The more alliteration you have, the sexier your speech will sound. To refine your speech, take a look at the script and replace words with their synonyms so that they form alliterations. Visit thesaurus.com for reference.

# CHAPTER 3.

# Speech Delivery

*In which you'll learn every essential aspect of speech delivery such as eye contact, gestures, movement, stance, voice modulation and much more*

## 18. I know my content very well, so do I really need to care about anything else?

The short answer is "Yes." You may know your content but you might not be aware of your *miscommunication*. Do you ever exhibit any of the following while making a speech?

- Hand shivers

- Wobbling of legs

- Repetitive gesturing of hands

- Walking left and right like a pendulum

- Shifting weight of body on right or left leg at regular intervals

- Slouchy shoulders

- Looking down at the floor

- Looking up at the ceiling

- Looking around and not making eye contact at all

- Monotone voice

- Showing tension in face while narrating a pleasant experience

- Laughing before the audience laughs at your jokes

- Not showing the emotion that corresponds to your message

- Mumbling

- Speaking too fast

- Not ending your words succinctly, especially those ending in -ing or -tion

If you do any of the above, you need to work on your delivery skills. Do you have a video recording of any of your talks? If so, use the video to identify the areas of distraction in your speech delivery and use the simple strategies outlined in the following sections to eliminate them.

## 19. How should I move during the presentation?

Before getting into movement, I want to talk about posture. Have you seen people speaking with slouchy shoulders and sunken chest? I am pretty sure you might have formed conscious or unconscious opinions on them. Have you seen people speaking with a straight back, straight head (as if having a crown on the head) and a solid stance? If not, observe the way Barack Obama speaks. Even before you speak, your posture will make a huge difference. Hence straighten your back and head, broaden your chest and shoulders and stand with firm footing. This posture will communicate nothing but *confidence*.

Now, let's talk about movement. Have you seen speakers who move from side to side without any purpose during a speech? Did you find it distracting? I used to get confused on movement. After the learning curve, I realized that speakers should *move only when they want to communicate an idea*. Movement helps in the following areas.

**Transition**: I have observed that movement can be used to transition from one point to another. We covered a few examples for movement in the transition section. Let us take a new example. Suppose you are giving a business presentation about a product's past and future releases. You can use movement as a transition tool. Standing at point A, you can talk about product version 1.0, then move to point B and talk about product version 2.0 and then move to point C and talk about future version 3.0.

**Drama**: You can use movement to depict the actual movement that happened in a scene. You can move to depict the drama in a story. For example, in our case study, I said the following.

> Mr. Jim has mastered the art of closing the sale. He asks three questions.
>
> "Did you like the meeting?"
>
> "Yes."
>
> "Would you like to be a member?"
>
> "Yes."
>
> "Is there anything stopping you from becoming a member?"
>
> "Um... I do not have cash."
>
> "I'll accompany you to the ATM machine."

During the last sentence, I *actually walked as if Jim* was accompanying the guest to the ATM.

**Increase Impact:** By moving, you can increase the impact of your speech. By putting a strong foot forward, you convey it is an important and strong point. By taking a step backward, you convey it is a vulnerable point. For example, in the case study, when I introduced the lessons – "Give solid support to someone in need" or 'Selling is not hard" or "Be passionate in what you do," I just took one step forward. Of course, it was coupled with expressions, gestures and other non-verbal behavior. But movement helped in increasing the impact.

## 20. How do I make effective eye contact?

Yes, we all know that eye contact with the audience during a presentation is important. However, having effective eye contact requires some skills. Let me ask you this. Have you observed someone while they were presenting?

I am pretty sure you would have seen one of the following scenarios:

1. The speaker is gazing all around the room except at the audience.

2. The speaker is looking at the audience but not really taking time to connect with the listener.

3. The speaker is talking with the audience by looking at one person (or one section if it is a large group) to complete a sentence and then moving on to another person in another section.

The above scenarios are based on the skill level of the speaker in increasing order where three is the highest. Every speaker starts from the first level. If you want to reach level three, here is the step-by-step procedure.

<u>Specific Steps for Effective Eye Contact:</u>

1. While practicing your speech, close your eyes; imagine your audience in your mind. Divide your audience into quadrants and number them from one to four – the order is up to you. Imagine talking to one person in first quadrant. Look that person in the eye and talk for 5 to 10 seconds.

2. Then, move on gradually to another person in the second quadrant and talk for the next 5 to 10 seconds.

3. Then, move on gradually to a person in the third quadrant and talk for the next 5 to 10 seconds.

4. Move on to the fourth quadrant and talk to someone there for 5 to 10 seconds.

5. Now repeat the whole cycle but with a different set of people from each quadrant.

6. Open your eyes.

7. Repeat this exercise regularly when you are doing your practice.

If you really do this exercise sincerely, your eye contact will improve by leaps and bounds and give you a natural connection with your audience.

## 21. Is there a simple way to improve the quality of my voice?

If content is your vehicle, voice is your fuel. Speaking happens because of your *voice*. Even if you have the perfect content and perfect body language, if you do not have a decent voice, your presentation will be a loss. If you received feedback on your voice, did you hear terms such as pitch, intonation, depth, exaggeration, etc.? I won't get into those terms here since it is beyond the scope of this book, but the following directives will ensure you'll have a great voice.

**How to Sound Clear**: Even after I had been speaking three or four years, the audience could not hear me properly. I thought it was because of low volume. When I dug deeper, I realized that my words were not clear.

As a speaker, the first and foremost duty is to speak every word with clarity. I hired a voice coach to correct my enunciation. After spending $200 for an hour's session with a voice coach, it dawned on me that I am dashing words as I speak. The session proved to be a game changer for me. Here are the specific areas on which you have to focus during practice:

- Make sure you pronounce every syllable of every word in your speech.

- Complete every word before you go on to the next word.

- Make sure you enunciate the endings of the words properly, especially words ending with -tion, -ing, -th, -er.

- Make sure you maintain breath and energy throughout the sentence. In other words, do not start off your sentence in high energy and end the sentence in low energy.

**How to Find Your Optimum Tone**: Most of the time, we speakers do not use sufficient volume to speak. We should be neither too loud nor too soft. We need to use our optimum tone to speak. This means our voice should be resonant and loud enough for our audience to connect with us. Below are the steps to find your optimum tone. This exercise will also free you from vocal blocks.

Initially, practice your speech in a tone that you would use to speak to a friend. Then, gradually increase your tone from soft to loud. At one point, you will feel that your voice seems natural and resonant, and that's your optimum tone my friend.

**How to Control the Pace of Your Speech:** In order to make it easy for listeners, we also need to speak at proper pace. The human ear can grasp words easily when spoken at a range of 120 to 160 words per minute.

As a first step, find out your current pace of the speech. Start a timer, start reading the content and stop the timer after 1 minute. The number of words you uttered will be the pace of your speech. If your pace falls within 120 to 160 words, you should be good. If not, you need to work on speaking within this range.

On a side note, certain parts of the speech work great if spoken slowly. Certain parts of the speech work great if spoken swiftly. While you practice, try experimenting with different paces for different parts of the speech. At one point, you will *feel* the right pace.

**How to Pause Effectively:** As silence between the notes creates a great piece of music, *pauses* between your spoken words add beauty to your speech delivery. Pauses are the most under-worked skill in speech delivery. A pause has multiple applications. A pause:

- Helps you to connect with the audience before the speech opening.

- Builds anticipation for your audience before you deliver the punch line for the joke.

- Gives time for the audience to laugh after you deliver the punch line for the joke.

- Acts as a signal that you are going to say something very important.

- Gives time for the audience to reflect on an important point.

- Acts as a transition tool for moving from one point to another.

The only way you can master pauses is by practicing – you'll have to intentionally give the pause even if you are practicing alone. Proper use of pauses will differentiate an amateur speaker and a professional speaker.

**How to Use Emotion**: Even if you did not remember anything till now (I hope not!), remember this: emotions make your audience take action. Earlier, we discussed pathos and the importance of emotions. That's the WHY. Now, let's talk about the HOW.

The following strategy will help your audience to feel the emotion. Write this down. *Feel the emotion in your heart before you express it through words.* I am not talking about melodramatic emotions, but instead about genuine feelings of joy, happiness, frustration and disgust. If you want your audience to feel the emotion of happiness, you should also feel the happiness; if you want your audience to feel the emotion of sadness, you should also feel the sadness. If you apply this simple technique, you will be awesome on stage. Try this when you speak next time. If it is a corporate setting, you can tone it down. If it is a community setting, you can feel free to express the emotions you feel. Hollywood actors do this, why not you?

If you want to master this critical area, you can refer to Emote by Vikas Jhingran. Vikas is an amazing speaker who is the 2007 World Champion of Public Speaking. In his book, he teaches how to give speeches with strong emotional content that will leave a lasting impact on the audience.

**How to Say Dialogue or Monologue:** If you remember, we discussed use of active voice when we talked about content refinement. In a speech setting, you'll often use active voice in the form of a dialogue or a monologue. If you are going to say a monologue or a dialogue, you need not mimic the person. However, you can use the *emotion* and *attitude* of that person. For example, Tony Robbins in his TED talk (*Why we do what we do*) says: "People say to me, 'I don't need any motivation.' And I say, 'Well, that's interesting. That's not what I do.'" The sentence "I don't need any motivation" is said in a harsh and loud voice to indicate the attitude of the person who spoke to Tony.

You also can say an effective dialogue by mirroring the attitude of the person saying the dialogue in your story or your experience. If you are a guy, this applies even for female characters in your story. You need not use a shrill voice to mimic a lady. You only need to show the attitude of a lady in the scene of your experience or your story.

You don't need mimicking talent to use a dialogue or monologue; however, you have to *clearly distinguish* the characters.

## 22. How do I use my hands during the presentation?

The term that describes the use of hands is "gesture." If you have not asked this question, I am certain this question will come up in future. Using hands was one of the problems I faced when I was learning mechanics of speaking. There can be multiple classifications under gestures. For simplicity, we'll classify gestures into two types: *emphatic gestures* and *non-emphatic gestures.*

**Emphatic Gestures:** Emphatic gestures are the movements to empha-size any point. They are the ones that accentuate your point by let-ting your natural emotions stroke at certain words. Pumping the fist of one hand into the open palm of other hand *to show how strong you feel,* opening up both hands *to invite your audience,* swaying your hand away from your body *to show denial* are all examples of emphatic ges-tures. The following are the mechanics of using your fingers/palm/hand for emphatic gesturing.

- Keep your fingers straight or slightly curled.

- Use open palm gestures. You should show your palm to the audience. By doing this, you build trust with your audience. Please take care that you do not point at the audience.

- Your hands should move from shoulder level instead of elbow level. This is one of the key differences between amateur speakers and professional speakers.

- Hands should stroke at the right word. Stroking before or after the intended word will seem artificial and distracting.

**Non-Emphatic Gestures:** Non-emphatic gestures help you describe an object/character, prompt the audience or depict the scene. Indicating 1-2-3 using fingers, raising one hand above your head to indicate ap-proximate height of a person, extending your hand to show the size of an object, prompting the audience to raise their hand are examples of non-emphatic gestures.

In day-to-day conversation, we use emphatic and non-emphatic ges-tures seamlessly. Don't believe me? Observe yourself when talking to your friend or a colleague. You'll know what I mean. But when it comes to public speaking, we get self-conscious and do not gesture in a natural way. Hence, we need some practice and preparation. Gesturing needs careful practice, or else it'll look canned and artificial.

Strategy for gesturing:

Practice till you internalize or have your speech in muscle memory. Once your script is in your muscle memory, video-record your speech. Observe how your hands move. Note the intended gestures as well as the distracting gestures. Then, practice to stop the distracting gestures and make sure your intended gestures seem natural and smooth.

You should also be comfortable enough on stage that you do not feel the need to gesture. Not gesturing (keeping your hands to the side) can add impact to certain parts of your presentation. Learning to speak without any gesture is a great skill to master. If you keep practicing this craft, you'll learn this.

## 23. How to create correct facial expressions during the presentation?

Let us talk about facial expressions. You might have heard the phrase "The face is the index to the mind." I am pretty sure you understand that the expressions in your face communicate a lot more than what you say verbally. Even though we know it, I think it is an area that we do not focus on enough when we present. Why do I say this – record yourself and watch your talk? Do you have natural facial expressions that agree with what you say? Our expressions are natural when we speak one to one. However, when you are on an elevated platform, the anxiety may not allow you to be natural. Though we can plan every expression, it will be extremely hard to sequence the expressions in a natural manner. For reference, I would recommend you watch Jim Key's 2003 Championship speech "Never Too Late" to study expressions.

In order to have natural facial expressions, there is a simple strategy: Practice the content till you get it into your muscle memory, and then consciously allow the *emotions to flow on your face*. You might have heard this before, but I am telling you to use this again and again because having your speech in your muscle memory is the key to unlock the delivery mechanics of public speaking.

Just to reiterate; a speech is said to be in your muscle memory when you don't have to focus on your next thought or word during the actual speech presentation. Having your speech in muscle memory has lot more advantages but one main advantage is that you will have natural and smooth expressions on your face.

# CHAPTER 4.

# Preparation Steps

---

*In which you'll learn strategies for connection, use of humor, venue setting, 20-step practice checklist   and much more*

---

## 24. How can I create and maintain my connection with the audience?

I am sure you have heard or used the term "connection." For example, some said, "I felt a connection with him," 'or 'I did not connect with him." If you have read the earlier sections, you might relate to what I am going to say. It was an aha moment for me when I realized that when people talked about creating connection, they were talking about ethos. The sooner the audiences feel your credibility, the more instant your connection will be.

Imagine a scenario where your friend is introducing you to his or her friend. How would you converse with the new person? Remember, you just got introduced. Would you say, "What are your goals in life?" or in a very loud voice say, "Hiiiiiiiii. Howwwww arrrrre yooouu?" You wouldn't say either. Ideally, you would just be more open. Let the other person feel comfortable. You might talk about things that are common: same school, same place you lived, same movie star you like or dislike, etc. Then, maybe crack a light joke or two. The new person might start to respond positive-ly. If this happens, you just started the connection. Why did this happen? The other person liked you and started trusting you.

The same scenario also applies to public speaking. You have to be open, authentic and credible in the eyes of your audience. Only then will you start building rapport, which will make you ready to connect with the audience.

**Six Practical Tools for Creating a Connection:**

**1. Your Introduction**: In most instances, you will be invited to present on stage by an anchor or a master of ceremonies. If you are talking to a new audience, then your introduction plays a crucial role to build likeability and trust. It is your responsibility to share your introduction in a way that covers the following points.

- What expertise you bring to the table or in other words – why you are qualified to speak.

- Care should be taken that it does not involve ego boasting such as speaker "climbed Mt. Everest in one hour," speaker "has a triple Ph.D.," speaker "ran a 10-mile marathon in 2 minutes," etc. The examples are extreme forms but I hope you got the idea.

- How you can help your audience.

- An interest apart from the topic or any light remark (good to have).

Take the following introduction as an example: "There is a concept and method by which you can create a joke. Once you know this, you can bring life into your presentations. The concept and method has helped our speaker to be among the top entertaining speakers at the national level. And today he is going to teach us 'How to Create Humor.' He likes jaywalking in Times Square and eats cupcakes when he gets stressed. Are you ready to listen? Please join me in welcoming Mr...............".

**2. Use the Pronouns You/We:** I learnt this tool from 1999 World Champion of Public Speaking Craig Valentine. The idea is to have as many "You" focused sentences as possible. Let me explain. When we speak, we bring our own experiences and achievements to the table and there is a tendency to use "I." While creating content, you need to frame it in such a way that you transition and involve the audience using "You" or "We" focused sentences so that they understand that you care about them. In fact, if you had noticed, I tend to use more "You" or "We" focused sentences even in this book.

**3. Speak In the Third Person**: Whenever you use "I," think twice. Unless it is your own original thought, realization, finding, experience or learning, do not use "I." If the idea or teaching is someone else's, use him or her in the reference. For example, when talking about ethos, logos and pathos, I clearly mentioned that it was a concept coined by Aristotle. My job is only to simplify and spread the information. This helps in establishing your credibility.

**4. Be Sincere**: Sincerely add value to your audience's life experience. Adding value could vary based on the purpose of your speech. If you are there to entertain them, give your 100% in entertaining them. If you are there to train them for project management skills, empower them to become the best project managers. If you are there to inspire them, genuinely help them to achieve greater things in life.

**5. Maintain Genuine Eye Contact**: Eyes are doorways to form connection. Not only in public speaking but also in one-on-one communications, we form connections through our eyes. While presenting, there is a tendency for your eyes to glaze over the audience, but the moment you talk *with* an audience, you develop a deeper bonding. If you want to know the mechanics, please refer to question #20.

**6. Engage Your Audience**: If your presentation has scope, you can use audience engagement to keep your audience interested throughout your presentation.

When you involve someone, they will listen to you all day long. Engage your audience with the following ideas.

Ask interactive questions: By asking interactive questions, you get immediate feedback on your audience's understanding of your subject. You can create a pop quiz, ask questions about them or ask questions about what you just explained. For example, in our case study, we had engaged the audience members by asking how many countries they had traveled.

Invite a few of them to the stage: This is a great technique if you are conducting workshops or training sessions. This way you have caught the attention of all the members because one of them is hanging out with you in the spotlight (so to speak).

Create a group activity: By doing this, the audience members interact with each other and work as a team. This works great for workshops or training sessions.

## 25. Is there a particular strategy to ensure that the audience will continue to listen?

If you can connect with your audience, they will listen to you all day long. However, if you are just looking for one strategy in particular that'll ensure an audience will continue to listen to you, then, EN-TERTAIN! I have seen hundreds of speeches, and unless it is a eulogy or crisis situation, an audience wants to be entertained. If you entertain well, your audience just can't stop loving you. When they love you, they listen to you. (Now please do not confuse your audience with your significant other. That person may love you but might not listen to you!)

Entertaining your audience does not mean telling laugh-out-loud jokes. And looking for jokes on the Internet is the last thing you should do. Those jokes will not reflect *you*. It won't be your personality speaking. Your best bet would be to use personal stories. Your audience will love you if you use personal stories which have clean humor.

Understanding the mechanics of humor is beyond the scope of this book. If you wish to quickly learn how to create humor, you can access my free report "Humor Creation Made Simple: Learn Humor in 30 Minutes" which covers ideas to create humor, joke structure, delivery of joke to live audience, practice exercise for you to identify different elements of humor and use of rule of three to create humor. You can download this exclusive report at: http://www.PublicSpeakKing.com/37steps.

One strategy for those who want to try their hand at humor is self-deprecating humor. It is nothing but making fun of yourself. Do not think by using self-deprecating humor, your self-respect will go down. In fact, the audience will respect you more because you are ready to let your guard down and poke fun at yourself.

Let us take real-time examples.

During a corporate town hall, our company executive vice president said: "I said to my wife that I am going to lead the new business unit in the company. She said, 'Okay.' I said, 'Aren't you excited?' She responded by saying, 'Whatever? Tell me, will you get more money or not?'"

Not sure if you chuckled but people laughed because he was the vice president, yet he was ready to make fun of himself.

In our case study, I said the following.

Later in the year, I competed in my first humorous speech contest. Somehow, I crossed the 3rd level of contest. People were saying things like, "You did not win because you were funny. You won because others were less funny."

People laughed because I was making fun of myself.

Take a moment and consider what amusing stories you have to tell. I am sure you have tons of stories to share. Self-deprecating humor increases your likeability quotient. Trust me, self-deprecating humor is a ninja weapon to break the psychological barrier between you and your audience.

A word of caution – you could face a situation where you were expecting the audience to laugh and they might not laugh. I am telling you beforehand that it might happen.

There are two ways to handle it. If they really did not understand that your intention was to create humor, then keep it going as if nothing happened. However, if they understood that your intention was to create humor and they did not laugh (this is tough!), then you can say something like "By the way, that was a joke." Usually, you will get a good laugh if you say it properly. If not, you might get a chuckle or smile. Whatever the result, never ever say anything negative about the audience because they did not respond as expected. In fact, stay away from saying anything that might affect your audience's sentiment in an adverse way.

When you are presenting in a business environment, you might feel a little uncomfortable in creating humor. It is okay. It is preferred not to create humor in serious business presentations. However, in the case of corporate town halls, account gathering, team gathering, etc., you can think about amusing stories from your workplace. Ask yourself: What amusing things happened while you achieved that stiff deadline? What fun things you do as a team? Be comfortable and genuinely amused when you entertain your audience. Your audience will catch that frequency pretty quickly and be hooked to every word.

## 26. What is the final checkpoint, before I freeze my content?

For a presentation, we use either verbal (words) or non-verbal (body language, visual aids) communication. The problem comes when we start rambling with too much information or we use too many strategies. Unlike written prose, speaking to an audience only gives you one chance to be heard. By far I think the most important part in your content preparation is the CLARITY of your presentation.

Questions that'll help you with clarity:

- Will I achieve my objectives?

- Is the purpose clear enough for my audience?

- Is my opening/context setting obvious?

- Are my supporting points relevant and tuned with my key points?

- Are my transitions clear?

- Is the summary and conclusion satisfactory?

- Is my voice easy to understand and hear?

- Am I enunciating all words properly?

- Do my stories get my point across?

- Do my non-verbal movements communicate my intended meaning?

The questions are endless, but I hope you got the idea. If any of your answers to the above questions are "No," then you need to work on that particular aspect. Before you freeze your content, be sure that the entire speech is CLEAR.

**A Tool to Improve Clarity:** I learnt this tool from an audio lesson by Lance Miller, 2005 World Champion of Public Speaking. He is an amazing speaker. He talked about a concept that increased my focus on my clarity aspect. He talked about "Painting the Picture" for the audience. Lance says that it is important to paint the audience's mind with the same picture that you are seeing in your mind. As communicators, our aim is to transfer the picture we have in our mind to our audience's mind. One way to create clear content is to look at each verbal and non-verbal aspect of our presentation and ask: "If I am in the audience, will this sentence or action paint the exact picture that I have as a speaker?" If the answer is "yes," keep the sentence; if not, chuck it out. This tool will help you to find the right elements and chuck out the unnecessary ones.

## 27. Can the venue affect my presentation?

Venue plays an important role in the success of your presentation. If you have direct access to it, work with the presentation planner well ahead of your actual presentation day on the following points.

**Six Factors at Venue That Can Affect Your Performance:**

**1. Venue Type:** Is your setting going to be in boardroom style where the approximate audience number will be somewhere from 10 to 40? Is the setting going to be classroom style where approximate audience size will be somewhere from 40 to 100? Is the setting going to be in an auditorium style (ideal for large audience, greater than 100)? *Knowing this will help you visualize the venue while you are practicing.*

**2. Time Limit:** Do you have a time limit? Are you going to be timed by someone in the audience or will you manage it by yourself? These questions will help you prepare your presentation from time limit perspective. You can cut down the number of words depending on time limit. For example, if you have been given 10 minutes, then you can plan to have 1200 to 1400 words based on the rate of your speech. You can also be prepared for any emergency ending, just in case you are asked to speak for less time.

**3. Projector:** If you are using Microsoft PowerPoint or Apple Keynote, or any digital visual aid, check if the venue has a projector. If not, make sure you have alternatives such as chart boards. You can also buy a pocket projector if that'll help you. PK301 PICO projector is a good option.

**4. Audience Seating Position:** They can be in boardroom style, conference room style or dinner table style. Boardroom is where there is a big table and the audience sits around the circumference of the table. Conference type is where seats are arranged in rows and columns. Dinner table style is where the audience sits around circular dining tables. From personal experience, dinner table style is not a good setup from the speaker's point of view. The reasons are:

- The audience is not seated in a pattern for making connection through eye contact.

- The audience seems scattered and the energy is unevenly spread across the venue.

How to have audience seating work to your advantage? Ask the meeting planner to put out only as many chairs as per the confirmed participation. The remaining chairs can be stacked and can be added if more people turn out. The rule of thumb is – *never leave empty chairs for a presentation*. Energy dissipates in emptiness. On the other hand, if the chairs/tables are close, there is a sense of connection and energy in the room, which will boost the overall atmosphere of the venue.

**5. Acoustics:** Acoustics of the venue matters. A venue with good acoustics will transmit sound clearly so that it is easy for the listener. If you have a chance, you can check the acoustics beforehand. If you are not happy with the acoustics and you have a choice, you can check with the presentation planner for a workaround.

**6. Audibility:** As your audience size increases, you need to take care of another critical factor, which is your AUDIBILITY. Don't worry if you do not have a low, deep and a resonant voice. We have tools such as a MICROPHONE to solve this issue. With a midsize audience setting, use of a microphone is optional. To determine if a microphone is necessary, run a simple test. Go the venue before the presentation date. Ask your friend or colleague to sit in the corners of the venue. Speak in your normal voice. If the room acoustics are good, you will be audible to your friend. If not, you need to use a microphone.

Check if you have a microphone facility at the venue. Think about which microphone is suitable for you. Is it a clip-on microphone or a handheld mike? If you are not comfortable with a handheld mike, then ask the planner to arrange a clip-on microphone. If you are using a clip-on microphone, folks might clip it on your suit collar. I would not recommend it because your voice might get distorted if you use amplified gestures. I would recommend clipping the microphone between the first and second button of your shirt.

## 28. Can you give me the exact steps to practice my speech?

You know, at a high level, public speaking seems to be a simple process. You speak and your audience listens. Is it that simple? Maybe it is not. That's the reason I have created a simple step-by-step process, which will act as a one-stop reference for your practice. As you progress down the steps, do not forget to incorporate the lessons of the earlier steps.

**20 Steps for an Effective Practice Session:**

1.  Stand straight with firm footing. Keep your spine and head straight.

2.  Keep your hands at your sides with your fingers slightly curled.

3.  Keep your feet at around 8 to 12 inches distant from each other.

4.  At this point, you need not worry about eye contact, gesturing, movement, facial expressions or voice modulation.

5.  Practice your speech content till it smoothly rolls off your tongue. Certain sentences or words might not be rolling off smoothly. Go back to your content and change the words or sentences that are not rolling off smoothly. You can keep doing this activity throughout your preparation phase.

6.  Check for any distracting mechanisms in your current speech. Use the list of mannerisms given in Q #18. If you find any, work on removing them by practicing for specific non-verbal or verbal behavior.

7.  As a next step, practice by speaking your content in loud, soft, slow and at last in a fast tone. While doing so, care should be taken that you also enunciate (make sure you end the words properly, saying each syllable of every word) the words clearly. By doing this step, you will clear vocal blocks, sound clear and use optimum tone.

8.  Complete every word before you go to the next word.

9.  Check if you are not starting the sentences in high energy and ending in low energy. If the content demands it, it's okay. However, if it is a regular pattern, practice to break that pattern.

10. Start focusing on internalizing your speech. You should be able to tell the content even if someone wakes you up in the middle of the night. This is the concept of muscle memory.

11. If you are planning to pause at certain places in your talk, then practice those pauses deliberately.

12. Feel the emotion in your heart and practice. If your content should make your audience feel happy, you should also feel the happiness. If your content should get your audience excited, you should also be excited.

13. Ask your friend to give feedback on relevance of your facial expressions to the intent of your speech.

14. Work on your eye contact using the visualization strategy explained in section #20.

15. Let your hand gestures flow naturally. Practice the following rules of thumb:

    - Use open palms.

    - Do not point at the audience.

    - Move hands from shoulder level.

    - Stroke at right word.

16. Work on your movements. Check your footwork; determine at what point of the stage you would be at different parts of your presentation.

17. If you are using PowerPoint, practice by sequencing the slides. You can practice by asking your friend to navigate the slides for you. Alternatively, you can use a remote control for the same.

18. Now, rehearse by incorporating all the steps. This is the challenging yet exciting part. At one point, you will feel powerful and excited. This is when you know you are evolving as a successful speaker.

19. Give a complete rehearsal to your close friends, family or anyone who would listen to your presentation.

20. Keep repeating the steps and fine-tune your presentation.

The above strategies are not something specific to a newcomer. They will work and help you, even if you are a fairly seasoned speaker. I have learnt that the above steps are kind of THE work you need to do if you really want to speak like a PROFESSIONAL.

## 29. Can you give me a strategy for not going blank on stage?

Going blank on the stage is one of the main fears of public speaking. If you follow the answers given in this book, you should not go blank. However, let's talk about it.

There is general advice such as "You should not over prepare your presentation." Well, the reason for this advice – you might look scripted or artificial. Moreover, you can easily go blank if you do not recall the script word by word. But that is generic advice.

We are talking about specificity. I think you should over prepare your presentation. When I say, over prepare, I mean drill (or internalize) the speech till the content becomes part of you. If I wake you up in the middle of your sleep and ask you to talk about your presentation, you should talk. We are not talking about storing it in memory.

We are talking about storing it in your muscles. *Your aim is to take your speech to* MUSCLE MEMORY. When you do this, there is genuine excitement. When you are at that state, there is no question of going blank. You will be telling yourself – "I can't wait to give my presentation." This is one of the simplest ways to get over your anxiety and sizzle on stage. You do this – I bet you will be excited to go to the stage.

# CHAPTER 5.

# Presentation Day Steps

---

*In which you'll learn how to dress, D-day checklist, handling last-minute butterflies, strategies to follow when you are live to audience and much more*

---

## 30. How to dress for my presentation?

If you think *I am there to speak – who cares how I am dressed*, you are completely wrong. You will turn off your audience even before you start speaking if you are not dressed or groomed properly. Unless you are a celebrity, you have to build rapport and credibility with your audience. It is not only about the attire but also about your grooming.

Once grooming is taken care of, the next item is to decide on the attire. How to choose the attire? Whether it should be business formal, or traditional/ethnic wear? A tip that can be applied to any situation – *always dress one step above the best-dressed person in your audience.* If most of the audience members are going to wear a blazer, then wear the best blazer. If hardly anyone is going to wear a blazer, then you can stick to business formals. If you are going to speak to an ethnic group and you are expecting them to come in traditional wear, then you can wear the best ethnic wear for your presentation.

**Pointers on Grooming/Dressing for Men:**

- Neatly trim your moustache (if you have one) and have a clean shave. If you have a beard, please trim it and shave the remaining real estate on your face.

- Neatly crop your hair, trim your nails and use a deodorant and/or light perfume.

- Shoes, Socks and Belt: If your shoes are brown in color, please wear them only with brown socks and brown trousers. If your shoes are black, please wear black socks. Black socks/shoe combination works for any trousers except brown trousers. If you are planning to wear black shoes and colored socks, please make sure the color of the socks matches the color of the trousers. Color of your belt should match the color of your shoe. Example: If you wear a black shoe, your belt also should be black in color.

- If your shirt is light in color, wear dark-colored trousers and vice versa. A neatly pressed light blue (or white shirt) shirt with navy blue (or dark grey) trousers, neatly polished black dress shoes with black socks, a formal black belt and a dress watch works like a charm. Brands such as Calvin Klein/Van Heusen work pretty well on quality as well as budget for shirts/trousers. Johnston & Murphy shoes and belts are awesome. They are a bit expensive, but the quality is worth it.

**Pointers on Dressing/Grooming for Women:**

- Trimmed nails and tied/combed hair looks classy.

- Mild cologne is also classy.

- Wear an outfit appropriate to the occasion.

Business formals work great for corporate presentations. A blouse (or blouse or sweater with blazer) with slacks/skirt should work well. A white top will go with navy blue/black trousers (or skirt).

Similarly, when presenting to a specific community, wearing an outfit that is familiar to them will work well.

- Color of footwear, handbag and belt should match. You probably won't use a handbag while presenting, but it is still good to know this tip.

- Choose simple accessories. A thin necklace, a watch on one wrist and a bracelet on the other will look neat.

- Heel height should be something you are comfortable wearing. Please do not use high heels if you do not wear them regularly.

- Wearing a tight outfit or something new is not recommended. It is more important to wear something comfortable.

## 31. Is there a checklist for the presentation day?

Having a to-do list before going to the presentation venue helps. Don't fret, it may seem like a lot, but once you get used to it, these things will become ingrained and second nature.

The following is a suggested to-do list before you start off to the venue. You can add your own points to the following list.

To-dos before going to the venue:

- Do eat light food. Breads and salads will work fine. You need energy to show energy in your presentation!

- Do charge your laptop beforehand. However, take your charger. If you have a PowerPoint presentation or videos to present, have a backup in a pen drive and in a DVD.

- Do take a cab/car instead of public transport if you are going from home. If you are going to drive your own car, then start early to avoid traffic jams and parking problems.

- Do hang around with a supportive friend. You need someone to bounce your content off. You will feel less stressful if there is a dependable person with you.

- Do reach the venue early.

To-dos after going to the venue:

- Do chat with the presentation planner and check the venue setting.

- Do check if the projector is working. If you have a PowerPoint presentation, try to display your presentation through the projector.

- Do check if you have a proper writing board and a working marker if you are planning to use the writing board.

- Do check for arrangement of chairs. Also, check if the number of chairs is in accordance with the number of people who have confirmed their presence.

- Do not forget to check the temperature set for air-conditioning. If change is needed, please work with the presentation or meeting planner.

- Do test the microphone for optimum sound. You can ask your friend or colleague to sit in different corners of the room and give feedback on your voice. Do this activity by placing the microphone at different levels of your tie or shirt.

- Do video-record your presentation. You can ask your friend to record. If you do not know anybody, ask the presentation planner to help you with this.

- Do check for any distraction because of the lighting. Are the lights falling on your eyes? Based on the scenario, take a call on whether you want the lights to be on or off during your presentation.

- Do remind the presentation planner or the anchor to ask the audience members to keep their cell phones on silent.

- Do not forget to hand over a copy of your introduction to the planner or anchor.

- Do not forget to reach out and greet your audience members as they enter the venue.

- Do converse with your audience after your greetings. Ask questions on what brings them there. Keep it quick and move on. It has to be natural.

## 32. What if my heart starts pounding, ears get heated and hands become cold, 10 minutes before the presentation?

This is possible. It used to happen with me for a long time. Even now I face this in certain scenarios. Scenarios could be:

- Giving a presentation for the first time at work

- Speaking at a conference where people who you respect and admire are in the audience

- Presenting your ideas for the first time to your senior management

- First-time interview of a celebrity or a VIP in your company or industry

- Speaking in a contest

- A proposal presentation which could win a big deal for your company

- A sales presentation which could sell your product to a large retailer

All the above scenarios can put you under a lot of pressure. I have been in a few of the situations. Even if you are not in a high-stakes presentation, you might face this situation. The following strategies work for me to tackle the last-minute anxiety at a physical and psychological level.

Steps to Tackle Last-Minute Anxiety at a Physical Level:

1. Rub your left palm with right hand for 10-15 seconds and vice versa. Do this for a few minutes till your heart rate comes to normal.

2. Slowly, breathe in and breathe out and get your heart rate to normal.

3. Sometimes, I go to a private corner where no one is around and do some vigorous punching and kicking in the air. This boosts up my energy and excitement. This has worked for me in high-pressure scenarios. I am sure a similar activity can help you too.

Steps to Tackle Last-Minute Anxiety at a Psychological Level:

1. Read through the following questions: *What is my intent? Am I present? Will I have fun? How would I give this presentation if I knew this was the last one ever?*

2. Take some time and genuinely answer them.

I learnt the above questions from 2001 World Champion of Public Speaking Darren Lacroix. The answers to the above questions will convert the last-minute anxiety into excitement. This is your ultimate aim. You have to get excited before taking the stage.

## 33. How do I carry myself from seat to stage, once the anchor calls my name?

The audience starts judging you from the moment you start walking towards the stage. So it makes sense to make the best of this opportunity that begins the moment you start from your seat and lasts till you make your first verbal or non-verbal communication.

Steps to Carry Yourself from Seat to Stage:

1. Get up from your seat and spring to the stage. You should show enthusiasm because it is contagious. The audience will catch your enthusiasm and will be eager to listen to you. Also, it is a great idea to wear a smile as you walk. By doing this, you are communicating the idea that you are happy to present to them.

2. As soon as you take position on stage, do not start off. The general tendency is to start off as soon as you come to the stage. I recommend against it. You should attract everybody's attention and create the connection before you start your speech. How

do you do it? Stand and scan the audience for a good 4 to 5 seconds. Meanwhile, your audience will stop doing other things and start focusing on you. Then, start off your presentation.

## 34. How do I handle myself during the actual presentation?

You have read so much. Do you think you have to remember and implement all the techniques, skills and ideas that we discussed till now?

No.

Yes, I said, "No." All that we learnt and studied will only be applicable through our preparation. The moment you take the stage, you should:

**Be Present:** Do not try to recollect word by word while you are speaking. You see, this is the mistake I used to make. The audiences want you to be *present* and talk to them. If you can remember one thing during your presentation, just be present and converse with your audience.

**Be Passionate:** You have read "be excited" quite a number of times. It boils down to being passionate about what you are going to say. When you love what you are going to say, your audience will be able to feel that love. That's why passion is a very important ingredient in success of a speech presentation.

**Be Energetic:** One of the laws of thermodynamics states that "Energy can neither be created nor destroyed. It can be transferred from one form to another." I think this applies to public speaking as well! Energy is neither created nor destroyed. It gets transformed from the speaker to the audience. Show energy in your presentation.

## 35. How do I handle any unexpected problems during the actual presentation?

During a live speech, situations could arise which were not planned. They can either fluster you or you can use them to your advantage. For example, in our case study I had asked people to raise their hands if they had traveled to more than 1 country, more than 2 countries, more than 5. When I kept going and reached 20 countries, I saw one hand still up and it was not Jim. I was wondering "Oh my God." To my amusement, I found he was a sailor (let us call him Bill) and it was his job to keep traveling to different countries! I said the following excitedly, "Oh, Bill is exempted. He traveled for work!" When I said that, the audience laughed and it was a good laugh because it was spontaneous.

The best possible way to handle problems is to be aware of the current situation. The #1 rule is *not to get flustered*. Know that your audience will empathize if there is a problem and always want you to do well. So, respect that and continue with your presentation.

Let us see the possible problems that you might face during your presentation.

**Losing Train of Thought:** While giving your presentation, you might lose your train of thought. It could happen because you saw someone and got distracted, or you were unsettled, or you were just anxious. If this happens, please do not kick yourself. I'll share the background story of our case study presentation. I was supposed to speak at 5:45 p.m. on a Saturday. The meeting started at 5 p.m. I started from my home, picked up a few friends and hit the road to the venue. However, I reached the venue parking at 5:42 p.m. (thanks for the insane amount of traffic!). I reached the meeting hall at 5:45 p.m. exactly before my slot. Before even I could adjust to the new climate, I started with my opening "I know Jim since 2009. At that time, he was a big man. Even now he is a big man, physically. To describe Jim in one line – Jim is like a 120-liter Coca-Cola bottle opening happiness wherever he goes." After that, I was supposed to say, "Jim did not pay me to say this. He is a great trainer and an awesome coach. You can contact him if you want coaching for prepared speeches, impromptu speeches or finding a girlfriend." Because of the hustle-bustle I lost my train of thought and missed it. However, I had a stock line to use. I said, "That's it. I am done." People laughed. It gave me time to get back on track. Then I continued with context setting. "Good evening, ladies and gentlemen, today, you are going to walk away with three lessons I learnt from Jim."

Strategies for bouncing back:

- Have some stock lines in place that can be used in case you lose your train of thought.

- Even if you forget, do not try to go back and share the missed portion. The joke I missed was a great one. However, I did not go back or try to force-fit the joke in the later part of the talk.

- Remember the structure, instead of words. If you do so, you'll know at which point of the presentation you were. Hence, you'll move on with your presentation.

**Power Shuts Down:** If power shuts down or PowerPoint does not work, just be cool.

This once happened in our corporate town hall. The entire power supply went off except for the microphone. The speaker said, "The microphone works. So, I will continue. My forehead can probably reflect the light you need." He was bald. The entire house erupted with laughter.

If you are halfway through the presentation and power shuts down, you can say, "I think we need a break."

You can also use this opportunity to say something light such as "So I will always be in the limelight" or "Was this is a plan to test my presentation skills?"

**Cell Phone Ringing:** This is a very common scenario. You can be prepared with an answer or two. If you feel it did not disturb the flow of your presentation, you can ignore it. If you feel it did, you can keep a few lines ready to create humor.

For instance, Craig Valentine in one of his audio programs used the following stock line: "Please tell your friend that I will call him later."

**Latecomer to Your Presentation:** Someone walking in late to your presentation is a common scenario. In that case, you can choose to ignore it and act as if nothing happened. This is a good idea if the person sneaked in without disturbing the flow of your presentation. In some cases, the late arrival might hamper the flow of your presentation. In such cases, you can tease around the person and create humor. Stand-up comedians use the following lines in such situations: "Welcome, we were just waiting for you" or "Do you need something... like a watch?"

## 36. How do I carry myself off the stage after my presentation?

Have you ever felt "when will this presentation end, I need to get off the stage"? In that case, you might have ended up – rushing through your talk and walking off in a hurry. Unfortunately, this is not going to help you in any way. In fact, the audience is observing you till you take your seat. I have tested the following steps as I have walked off the stage – they work like a charm!

Specific Steps to Carry Yourself Off the Stage:

1. After you say those last words of your presentation (example "Thank you"), pause, smile and say good-bye internally. The audience will understand even if you do not verbalize anything.

2. Pass on the control to the anchor or master of ceremonies.

3. While you turn and walk off the stage, show genuine enthusiasm. This conveys that you were happy to talk with the audience. The audience will get caught up in that enthusiasm and feel happy that they took the time to listen to you.

## 37. What should I do after the presentation?

Hurray…! Finally, you have successfully completed your presentation. Treat yourself with a hot cup of cappuccino! Now, you earned an experience. You will grow as a speaker not just by your experience but when you reflect on your experience.

Here are the directives to reflect on your experience.

**Get Audience Feedback:** Let's take a case where you'll ask for feedback from a person in the audience whom you do not know. Now, for example, you gave a speech at your corporate office. You break for refreshments or lunch and you make eye contact with someone who was in your audience. The conversation could go as follows.

You: "Hello, I am <your name>."

Audience Member: "Yes, we know you! I am <person's name>. You were great up there."

You: "Thank you. I really appreciate it. Can I ask you something?"

Audience Member: "Sure."

You: "If I could ask you one key thing you learnt from my presentation – what would it be?"

Audience Member: "I learnt…"

You: "Any one thing that could be done differently?"

Audience Member: "Yes, I felt you could have…."

You: "Thank you for your kind feedback. It was great talking to you."

Audience Member: "It was a pleasure. See you."

**Give Your Own Feedback:** Ask yourself: "What can be done better?" If you feel something needs improvement, you need to find the correct way of doing it. If you have access to an expert, reach out to him or her and ask for help. Depending on your relationship, you can take free or paid consultation.

Another alternative is to watch how super experts such as Barack Obama or Steve Jobs communicate. Obama's presidential acceptance speech "Yes, We Can" is an amazing reference for community style speaking. Jobs's keynote speeches for iPhone launches are amazing for corporate style presentations. Reverse engineering the techniques will be time-consuming but you will learn a ton of skills in the process.

**Analyze Your Video:** Do you remember, you asked your friend or colleague to record your video? Get hold of your speech recording. Darren Lacroix, 2001 World Champion of Public Speaking, has said that we will improve 2X from the current level if we just see our video recording and learn from our mistakes. If you forget everything and just apply this step, you will be far ahead in your speaking game.

<u>To-dos after collecting your speech video:</u>

1. Do mute the audio. Just watch the video and identify the exact areas of distraction in your non-verbal delivery. Following is the list of distracting mannerisms and strategies to overcome them.

- Hand shivers:

  Keep your hands forcefully to your side till your content is in your muscle memory. The more you practice in the right way, the better you will get.

- Wobbling of legs:

  Practice your content by distributing equal weight on your legs. The more experience you get on stage, the sooner it will fade away.

- Repetitive gesturing of hands:

  Keep your hands forcefully to your side while practicing your script. This needs practice. Refer to <u>the section on gestures, Q #22</u>.

- Moving left and right like a pendulum:

  Refer to <u>the section on movement, Q #19</u>.

- Shifting weight of body on right or left leg at regular intervals:

  Distribute equal weight between two legs and practice your content.

- Slouchy shoulders:

  While practicing, keep your spine straight. As a cross check measure, your chest should be out facing the audience.

- Not making eye contact with audience or looking at the ceiling:

  Refer to the section on practicing effective eye contact, Q #20.

- Showing tension in face while narrating a pleasant experience:

  Refer to the section on facial expressions, Q #23.

- Laughing even before the audience laughs after telling a joke:

  Refer to *Humor Creation Made Simple: Learn Humor in 30 Minutes*. You can access it from http://www.PublicSpeakKing.com/37steps.

- Not showing emotions that correspond to intent of the message:

  Refer to the section on adding emotions, Q #21

2. Do unmute the audio and minimize the video. Listen only to the audio and identify the exact areas of distractions in your verbal delivery. Following is the list of distracting mannerisms and strategies to overcome the same.

- Monotone voice OR mumbling of words and dashing of words:

  Refer to How to control the pace of the speech, Q #21

- Syllables such as -ing, -tion, -nd not enunciated properly:

  Refer to How to sound clear, Q #21

- Low voice without any energy OR sinusoidal modulation which is starting the sentence with high energy and ending the sentence with low energy:

  Refer to <u>How to find your optimum tone, Q #21</u>

Learn from the feedback, have fun and get excited for your next presentation.

# BONUS CHAPTER.

# Speech Script

---

*In which you'll access the script used as case study
in this book*

---

**Case Study Speech Script:**

<u>Title:</u> Lessons Learnt from Jim, <u>Time taken:</u> 7 min.

I know Jim since 2009. At that time, he was a big man. Even now he is a big man, physically. To describe Jim in one line – Jim is like a 120-liter Coca-Cola bottle opening happiness wherever he goes. That's it. I am done.

Good evening, ladies and gentlemen, today you are going to walk away with three lessons I learnt from Jim.

Let me talk about the first lesson. In 2009, a contest was in progress. Jim was the host. He asked the facilitator to close the door and stand out guarding the room. One empathetic audience member shouted, "Mr. Jim, he will miss the contest. This is not fair." In such a tense situation, what would you reply? I would have said, "Yes. Let me ask him to stand inside so that he can also see the contest" or something to support the cry. But Jim said those unforgettable words – "Yes, yes, he will miss the contest." Our audience member went speechless. No further comments.

Later in the year, I competed in my first humorous speech contest. Somehow, I crossed the 3<sup>rd</sup> level of contest. People were saying things like "you did not win because you were funny. You won because others were less funny." I wanted help. I reached out to many and finally Jim gave me a hug and said, "I will help you." He arranged for a mentoring session for one full day at my home. That day, Jim and a few others came to my home. You know what was the first question he asked, "What do we have for lunch?" I went, "Really?" However, the inputs and ideas that were discussed that day helped me cross the semifinals and be among the final 6 speakers in the entire district. The lesson – give solid support to someone in need.

Now, let me tell you about the second lesson. How many of you agree "Selling is hard"? Wrong. Why? When Jim is amongst us, it will be a sin to say that selling is hard. I can prove it in a minute. Why? How many of you can sell a print poster of a cheerleader at three times its cost price? If he can do that, converting a guest into a community member is child's play. I throw an open challenge. If anyone can prove that you are a better salesman than Mr. Jim, I will ask Jim to give you 1000 bucks as cash prize.

A guest coming into our community meeting has a need. All you are doing is closing the sale. And Mr. Jim has mastered the art of closing the sale. He asks three questions.

"Did you like the meeting?"

"Yes."

"Would you like to be a member?"

"Yes."

"Is there anything stopping you from becoming a member?"

"Um... I do not have cash."

"I'll accompany you to the ATM machine."

How easy was that? The lesson – selling is not hard.

The third lesson I learnt from Jim is to be passionate in what we do. Three years ago our city had only 8 to 10 clubs. Now, our city has more than 25 clubs because of his leadership. It could have never been done if it was not for his passion. Let me tell you one more thing.

How many of you have traveled to more than 1 country? How many of you have traveled to more than 2 countries? How many of you have traveled to more than 5 countries? How many of you have traveled to more than 10 countries? Here is a person who has traveled to more than 40 countries; however, I don't understand why he always travels alone. The lesson, be passionate in what you do.

Today, I want you to walk away with the three lessons that I learnt from Jim. They are – give support to the ones who need it, selling is not hard, be passionate in what you do.

I congratulate Jim on completing his 20-year tenure in our community and wish him all the best for the next 20 years.

# Conclusion

First of all, thank you for completing the book. Even though many won't bother to take the effort, you took the effort and time to learn these valuable skills.

Most people who have questions regarding public speaking would not know what you know. I am so excited that you took the effort to find those answers.

I don't know how you feel, but I feel excited whenever I help someone learn something new.

I have learnt that *being coachable* is one of the key traits that successful people show. You have shown that trait.

Going forward, there are two options.

You could just keep presenting the way you were doing or you can implement these simple strategies to sizzle on stage. You might not be able to incorporate all the ideas at one go. However, you can take one strategy at a time and implement them.

You'll face situations that demand your speaking skills. Trust yourself; you'll do well.

You know, the real thrill for me will be when you get results in your speaking game.

If the book has helped you in any way, I'd love to hear from you. Share your thoughts either to me (Rama@PublicSpeakKing.com) or in the review section of Amazon so that it'll help future readers.

Keep Smiling, Keep Rocking and Happy Public Speaking.


Wish You Success,

Ramakrishna Reddy

# Gratitude

I would like to thank all the kind people who have helped me learn the skill of public speaking. I would like to thank champion speakers Lance Miller (www.lancemillerspeaks.com), Darren Lacroix (www.darrenlacroix.com), Craig Valentine (www.craigvalentine.com), Dilip Abhayasekhara (www.drdilip.com) who helped me in one or another way.

I don't think I would have stepped up my game of speaking without my coach and mentor Jerry Aiyathurai. Jerry, you rock! I owe you a lot.

I am grateful to all the people whom I have mentored. Even I learn from the process as much as you do.

I am indebted to my dad, Narayana Reddy – thank you for giving me the freedom and wisdom. Mom, Ammayeammal – you are the best thing I could ever get. My three lovely sisters Leelavathy, Lakshmi and Indumathy – thank you for taking caring of me after mom left for heaven. My friends, teachers and colleagues at school, college and office – your unconditional love and friendship is a blessing.

Deepti Kizhakkeveettil and Shashank Sharma, thank you for your inputs. I could go deep into a reader's mind after your feedback.

My book editors, PJ Dempsey and Charisma Srivastava, thank you for taking this from one level to another level.

My final proofreader and editor Marcia Abramson, thank you so much for making it look professional and cool.

My book cover designer Kyle, you are awesome. My honest critic, Arun Prabhu – thank you for your constant support for this book.

*You*, the reader: this is exciting. This book would not hold any value without you! Thank you for trusting and investing your time.

Made in the
USA
Monee, IL